Getting Started in Emerging Markets

The Getting Started In Series

Getting Started in Online Day Trading by Kassandra Bentley
Getting Started in Asset Allocation by Bill Bresnan and Eric P. Gelb
Getting Started in Online Investing by David L. Brown and Kassandra Bentley
Getting Started in Internet Auctions by Alan Elliott
Getting Started in Stocks by Alvin D. Hall
Getting Started in Mutual Funds by Alvin D. Hall
Getting Started in Estate Planning by Kerry Hannon
Getting Started In Online Personal Finance by Brad Hill
Getting Started in 401(k) Investing by Paul Katzeff
Getting Started in Security Analysis by Peter J. Klein
Getting Started in Global Investing by Robert P. Kreitler
Getting Started in Futures by Todd Lofton
Getting Started in Financial Information by Daniel Moreau and Tracey Longo
Getting Started in Emerging Markets by Christopher Poillon
Getting Started in Technical Analysis by Jack D. Schwager
Getting Started in Hedge Funds by Daniel A Strachman
Getting Started in Options by Michael C. Thomsett
Getting Started in Real Estate Investing by Michael C. Thomsett and Jean Freestone Thomsett
Getting Started in Tax-Savvy Investing by Andrew Westhem and Don Korn
Getting Started in Annuities by Gordon M. Williamson
Getting Started in Bonds by Sharon Saltzgiver Wright
Getting Started in Retirement Planning by Ronald M. Yolles and Murray Yolles

Getting Started in

Emerging Markets

Christopher Poillon

John Wiley & Sons, Inc.
New York • Chichester • Weinheim • Brisbane • Singapore • Toronto

This book is printed on acid-free paper. ♾

Published by John Wiley & Sons, Inc.

Published simultaneously in Canada.

Cataloging-in-Publication Data is on file at the Library of Congress.

ISBN 0-471-39545-5

Printed in the United States of America

10 9 8 7 6 5 4 3 2 1

To my Mother, who has always been there for me.

Contents

Acknowledgments xi

Chapter 1

Why You Should Invest in Emerging Markets 1

They Didn't Teach This Stuff in Business School! 1

Safety Through Diversification 5

Buy Low, Sell High 7

You Can Make a Lot of Money 16

Chapter 2

The Players: The Emerging Market Index Funds 19

What Is a Fund, Anyway? 19

The Country Funds 23

The Asian Markets 26

Australia 27

China 30

Hong Kong 33

India 37

Indonesia 41

Japan 45

Korea 49

Malaysia 53

Pakistan 56

Philippines 59

Singapore 62

Taiwan 65
Thailand 68
Vietnam 72
The South American Markets 76
Argentina 77
Brazil 81
Chile 85
Mexico 89
Africa and the Middle East Markets 92
Israel 93
South Africa 96
"Developing" European Markets 99
Portugal 100
Russia 103
Spain 107
Turkey 110

Chapter 3

A New Toy: Investment Software 113
Time to Get Busy 113
Software 114
Nonprofessional Tools 119
Professional Tools 126
Financial Data Options 128

Chapter 4

Basic Stock Analysis 131
In the Beginning 131
Chart 132
Technical and Fundamental Analysis 135
Generic Indicators 137

Technical Indicators 141
Fundamental Indicators 152

Chapter 5

Investment Strategies and Other Important Stuff 155
Ready, Set, Go! 155
Your First Steps 157
Basic Time Strategies 161

Chapter 6

Online Brokers: Taking Control 173
It's So Easy! 173
Selecting a Broker 175
Taking a Closer Look 177
Online Broker Review 179
Buying and Selling 184
That's All, Folks! 189

Glossary 191

Index 199

Acknowledgments

First, I would like to thank various friends and family who volunteered their valuable time assisting with different phases of the project:

- ✔ Noel Cook, my uncle, who has spent zillions of hours proofing and editing my many written projects from film scripts to books
- ✔ Dennis Wholey, noted TV personality and best-selling author and friend, who has invested his time and wealth of knowledge advising me on my various media projects
- ✔ Chris Wright, psychotherapist and part-time investor, who provided initial creativity and insight

I was also very fortunate to enlist a friendly and effective agent—Muriel Nellis of Literary and Creative Artists, in Washington, D.C. Thanks also to her assistants, Leslie Toussaint, and her replacement, Jane Roberts. I never would have imagined that publishing a book could be so painless.

And finally, thanks to the staff at John Wiley & Sons—especially Debby Englander and Mary Todd—again, for making the publication of this book such an efficient process.

Getting Started in
Emerging Markets

Chapter 1

Why You Should Invest in Emerging Markets

THEY DIDN'T TEACH THIS STUFF IN BUSINESS SCHOOL!

In the early 1990s, I made a fortune buying *open-end funds* in the "developing countries" of Asia and Latin America. In the process, I developed a systematic process that you too can easily follow to safely reap the rewards that these *emerging markets* offer. Particularly now as we enter the new millennium, these markets are especially ripe for making significant amounts of money.

> **open-end fund** the same as a mutual fund. A closed-end fund often is incorrectly referred to as a mutual fund; but actually it is an investment trust.

You will be pleased to know that following my *investment* program for these country funds requires very little stock-trading knowledge. So whether you are a new investor or a sophisticated trader with years of experience, you can benefit from these strategies.

emerging market a financial market of a developing country, usually a small market with a short operating history.

investment an item of value purchased for income or capital appreciation.

My system was designed to require only 15 minutes a day to manage, much less if you take the long-term approach. So you will not even need to quit your day job in order to maximize your investment returns.

How did I gain this knowledge? It all started in college. . . .

I became a business major primarily because I wanted to be successful making lots of money. It seemed very logical: Most of the wealthy people I had heard of (at that time, I did not actually *know* anyone wealthy) made their money in one form of business or another. Oh, and then there were doctors, but that's another story.

So, in 1983, at the age of 17, I entered my university as a business major. It wasn't too long—after an accounting class or two—that I felt a bit bored and creatively unchallenged as a business major. But more important, they were not teaching me how to make money; they were teaching me how to make *other people* money.

After graduating, my wanderlust spirit started to take root, so I looked for graduate programs in business in exotic locations. I selected the University of Hawaii in Honolulu. Hawaii was a respected international business school, specializing in the Asia-Pacific region. And I even got a full teaching assistantship, with tuition waivers. Now I could finally learn to make money!

Well, you would not believe it: They do not teach you how to make money in graduate school either. As in undergraduate school, they teach you how to make other people money. In Finance, we learned how to calculate the "future value" of things. I never used any of this in business later—not even when I worked for a bank in Asia. In Managerial Accounting we learned about . . . you know, I cannot really remember. And Economics . . . well, we did learn about interest rates and inflation, but not how it applied to the real world.

So, I graduated with an MBA at the age of 23, and entered the real world to learn about business and how to make money.

After a year or so of working for a management consulting firm, first in Washington, D.C., and then in Toronto, I took the second big adventure of my life: I packed my bags and moved to Hong Kong and China in search of success and happiness. This would prove to be one of the most educational and interesting decisions of my life.

It was 1990, and the United States was entering a recession. As a relatively fresh MBA, I was not in great demand in the American workforce at the time. Young MBAs were the first to be cut from companies hit by the struggling economy. Europe was also hit hard. But Asia was booming. Not having secondary language skills, however, limited my choices. For example, Japan had its own MBA population and was a monolinguistic society. Hong Kong stood out among the Asian countries: highly capitalistic, American-friendly, English was a common second language, lax visa standards, and a desperate need of American management know-how. What a great opportunity to put my making-other-people-money skills to good use.

My second job in Hong Kong was where I first really learned about international finance and how to make myself money. I was hired as special assistant to the general manager of Standard Chartered Bank. Standard Chartered is a British bank with a long history in developing countries, particularly China and India. It was here, as the personal assistant to the bank's chief executive, that I got to see firsthand the daily operations of the bank's retail, corporate, treasury, stock broking, and private banking divisions. It also was here that I watched senior executives manage their own money from Reuter's terminals on their desks.

As you may know, Reuter's is an internationally respected news service, which sends live news, stock, and other financial information to special terminals for a *very* costly monthly fee (thousands of dollars, I believe).

I am very excited to tell you that now you and I can get most of this information free over the Internet. Later I will explain how you can receive live stock data at very reasonable monthly fees. This is a very special time for the personal investor.

It was also at this time that I jumped in and took my chances at stock market investments. My first risky investment was an $800,000 apartment I purchased with a loan from my bank; I quickly resold it at a profit a few months later. In 1990, without the Internet and online brokerage houses, if small-time investors like me wanted to get a piece of the action, we could do it through *mutual funds*. At the time, there were a handful of fund companies that specialized in open-ended emerging market mutual funds. (A little later I will discuss open-end and *closed-end funds* in detail). I took my profits from my real estate venture and invested them in India, China, Singapore—all of the booming Asian markets—through mutual funds.

> **mutual fund** an open-ended fund operated by an investment company that raises money from shareholders and invests in a group of assets, in accordance with a stated set of objectives. Benefits include diversification and professional money management. Shares are issued and redeemed on demand, based on the fund's net asset value, which is determined at the end of each trading session. A closed-end fund often is incorrectly referred to as a mutual fund; actually it is an investment trust.

In this process, I learned how to *leverage* my investments by taking *margin loans* from the fund companies. (I also will discuss these terms in greater length later.) For every dollar in profit I made, I took a loan out on it to invest more and more in these Asian funds. I made a fortune overnight. I was making so much money that I left my banking job so I could watch my money more closely. It was a very exciting time.

But then I learned a big lesson in life: What goes up, will eventu-

closed-end fund a fund with a fixed number of shares outstanding, and one that does not redeem shares the way a typical mutual fund does. Such funds often are listed on a major stock exchange and trade like other securities. Unlike a typical mutual fund, a closed-end fund's share price can trade above or below its net asset value.

leverage the degree to which an investor or business is utilizing borrowed money.

margin loan a loan to purchase securities provided by a broker to clients.

ally come down—especially stock markets. Being so new to the world financial markets, I did not realize that economies go up and they go down. Always, period. And they usually go down when everyone's getting rich, and no one expects it. After all, if we expected it, we could all get out in time. As I share with you these powerful lessons, you will see that we are entering possibly the most opportune time in history to make a fortune from stock investments in developing country funds.

But first, before I go into all of this good stuff, let me cover some other topics to explain why you should invest in emerging markets.

SAFETY THROUGH DIVERSIFICATION

"Emerging markets are risky," you say. Well, I personally do not agree, but many financial experts may. But one thing all financial experts, managers, and planners agree on is that everyone should have a *diversified portfolio*.

diversified portfolio a collection of investments all owned by the same individual or organization containing a variety of investments that are unlikely to move in the same direction.

Typically, *diversification* means having money invested in a variety of financial instruments: cash, *stocks*, *bonds*, real estate, and the like. The theory behind diversification is that we maximize our return over the long run by spreading out our risk. For example, some years stocks may perform poorly, yet the value of your home may rise. Or stocks dip and bonds go up. So, over the long run, your portfolio increases at a gradual rate (albeit a low rate if you follow typical investment strategies).

diversification a portfolio strategy designed to reduce exposure to risk by combining a variety of investments, such as stocks, bonds, and real estate, that are unlikely to move in the same direction at the same time.

stock an instrument that signifies an ownership position, or equity, in a corporation and represents a claim on its proportionate share in the corporation's assets and profits.

The most successful financial advisors recommend that people have a mix of international investments in their portfolios. Some experts would even suggest that at times, average Americans should have up to 50 percent of their portfolios invested in international financial instruments. If you think about it, this makes sense: When Asia was in a recession recently, America was in a *bull market*. And when I was living in Asia and Asian countries were thriving, America was in a *recession*.

bond a debt instrument issued for a period of more than one year with the purpose of raising capital by borrowing. The federal government, states, cities, corporations, and many other types of institutions sell bonds. A bond is generally a promise to repay the principal along with interest on a specified date (maturity).

bull market a prolonged period of rising prices, usually by 20 percent or more.

recession a period of general economic decline; specifically, a decline in gross domestic product for two or more consecutive quarters.

You will be surprised to know, however, that I have learned to make lots of money in emerging market funds in recessions *and* bull markets—and I will share these strategies with you later. (Other than property and cash, all of my money is invested in international instruments.)

So, to summarize, diversification is a good thing. And investing in emerging markets is a form of diversification.

BUY LOW, SELL HIGH

As a child watching television, occasionally I saw a Smith Barney ad for financial services. In one, a man rode a roller coaster up to the top, stepped off before it zoomed downward, and said something about buying low and selling high.

In reality, with typical American stocks, this is difficult to do. During normal market conditions, most stocks have low *volatility*. That is, they do not make dramatic jumps up and down. So there are few good buy-low opportunities. Of course we should have purchased Amazon and AOL when they were mere dollars per share. We would be rich today. At the time when they were low priced, however, their names and potential were unknown.

> **volatility** the relative rate at which the price of a security moves up and down; found by calculating the annualized standard deviation of daily change in price.

Investing in closed-end country funds in emerging markets provides a rich field of opportunities to buy at major lows and ride them up to their highs. The lows in these markets, as you will see, present much less risk than their American counterparts.

As an illustration, in 1999 the U.S. stock markets were at their peak—their highest in history. Remember: What goes up must come down! And I would not want to be in the U.S. market when it does crash.

I have learned that the signs of a future stock market crash can often be read. The market has hit a recent all-time high; then it makes major downs with moderate rebounds. The culprits are usually *interest rates* and *inflation*. At the market's peak, more people are buying expensive homes, cars, and jewelry.

> **interest rates** interest per year divided by principal amount, expressed as a percentage.

All of this brings flashbacks of my experiences in Asia before the major stock market crash and recession there.

inflation the overall general upward price movement of goods and services in an economy, usually as measured by the Consumer Price Index and the Producer Price Index.

Figure 1.1 shows the China Fund, which roughly follows Hong Kong's Hang Seng Index—the equivalent of the Dow Jones Industrial index in the United States. The rising trend line from January to December indicates how pleased investors must have been: The market doubled in a year! And it was not only investors in the Hong Kong stock market who thrived. Everyone's property value skyrocketed. There were Rolex stores on every corner, restaurants were packed, everyone was optimistic, and the economy was booming. Oh, and I was a very happy camper, too.

But now let us continue our story with Figure 1.2, which is a chart of the same fund, extended to the end of 1999. If you invested in

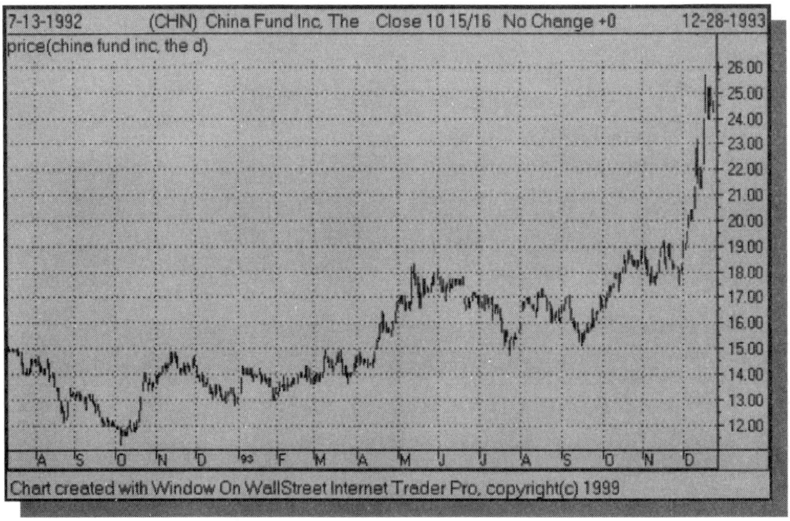

FIGURE 1.1 The China Fund, July 1992 to December 1993.

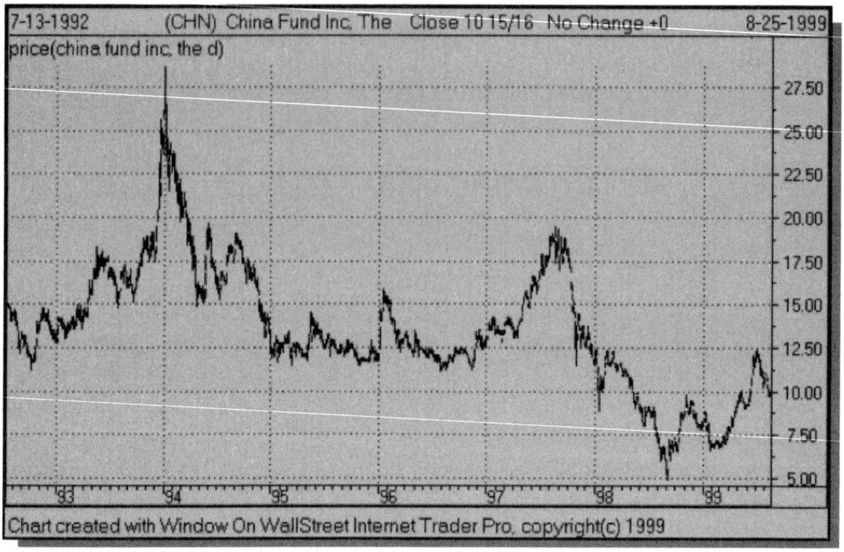

FIGURE 1.2 The China Fund, July 1992 to August 1999.

a Hong Kong/China fund near its peak, in a rush of excitement to benefit from the booming economy, even now you would not have recovered your money. Now *that's* risk!

Now let us look at Figure 1.3, a chart of a U.S. *stock exchange*, Nasdaq. It tells a similar story: a country and its people gaining dramatic wealth in a short period of time. (According to a recent *Washington Post* report, one eighth of the households nestled in high-tech country make more than $150,000 per year and have savings of over $500,000).

stock exchange an exchange on which shares of stock and common stock equivalents are bought and sold.

Note Nasdaq's dramatic rise on the figure. Look familiar? Now *that's* risk too.

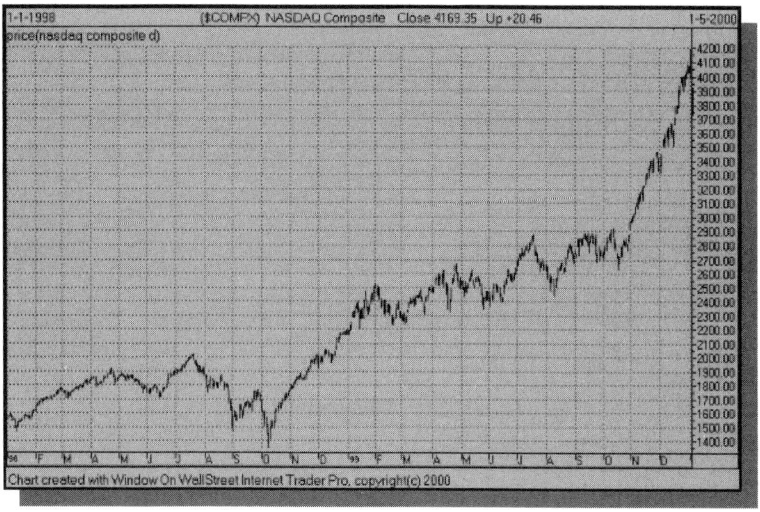

FIGURE 1.3 Nasdaq Composite Index, 1998 to 2000.

I can't predict where Nasdaq will go. It could double within the year—no one can forecast these things. But doesn't it remind you a bit of Asia in 1993/1994?

Now let us look back at Figure 1.2 from a different perspective. Since that time Asia has been in a long recession. It seems to be in the process of coming out of it as of now, and stock prices are quite low. Even if Asian markets drop further, most likely they will rebound in a short time. I believe Asian funds at this time are much less risky than American stocks and funds. There is less room to drop.

But one thing I can say with confidence: Emerging markets appear much less risky at this time than their American counterpart.

How could you *not* afford to invest abroad?

It's Easier Than You Think

A few years back, if a nonprofessional investor like you or I wished to purchase stock, we would have to get in our car, push off with our feet, go down to our Bedrock financial advisor, verbally place an *order*, a bird would fly to Rock Street with the order, and we'd have to pay outrageous transaction fees. Yabba dabba doo!

> **order** a request from a client to a broker to buy (buy order) or sell (sell order) a specified amount of a particular security or commodity at a specific price or at the market price.

Of course the reality was not that bad, but the description is not too far off either. Before online investment services developed, most people placed orders through their financial advisors. And, because stock information was not as readily available as it is today, the average personal investor could not make educated investment decisions. We really were at a major disadvantage; only the rich and powerful could buy and sell trades on a minute-by-minute basis.

Now that has all changed. Although the Wall Street elite still share inside information that you and I will never be privy to, our investment power is almost on a par with theirs: We can get the same news Wall Street gets as it is released, get tick-by-tick stock *quotes* in *real time*, and purchase stock in a few seconds—all over the Internet in the comfort of our homes, without burdensome financial advisor fees.

> **quote** the highest bid or lowest ask price available on a security at any given time.

> **real time** current, as with quotes or news; opposite of **delayed**.

Online investing may be intimidating to most Americans who have just started playing around on the Internet and always have relied on "professionals" to invest their money. But it should not be; it is very safe and very easy.

(By "safe," I mean that you can trust online brokers with your money; they have your investments insured by the government. But if you make crazy investment decisions, taking tips from your best friend's second cousin who knows someone who works on Wall Street, your money may not be very safe after all.)

In a later chapter I'll take you through the step-by-step processes of selecting stock *analysis* software, an online *broker*, selecting and placing orders to buy and sell stock, and how to monitor your portfolio. I will explain these processes in detail, to ensure that your jump into personal investing will be as trouble free as possible.

analysis the examination and evaluation of relevant information to select the best course of action from among various alternatives.

broker an individual or firm that acts as an intermediary between a buyer and seller, usually charging a commission. To sell securities and most other products, a license is required.

And, if you are like me, you will be disappointed to learn that monitoring your investments takes only 15 minutes a day, once you get started.

Control Your Own Destiny (Or, at the Very Least, Your Money)

I learned the hard way. When I was making handfuls of money back in Asia, eventually I was given my own private banker. Because my account grew to over $500,000, my account was transferred upstairs to the "private bank." Like many Americans, I now received financial advice from an investment "professional."

Around this time it finally dawned on me: The rich get rich not with their own money but with other people's money.

As shown in Figure 1.1, times were great—the Asian stock markets were at an all-time high. But then, in early 1994, when the market started to drop, you would hope that your financial advisor would caution you, and possibly suggest you take some money out for a while to see which way the markets would go. You would expect them to inform you that the recent decision by the *U.S. Fed* to significantly lower interest rates could have dramatic effects on Asian stock markets.

U.S. Fed the seven-member Board of Governors that oversees Federal Reserve Banks, establishes monetary policy (interest rates, credit, etc.), and monitors the economic health of the United States.

Well, I received no warnings at all. As my stocks tumbled and I lost a lot of my gains, my advisor, receiving her instructions from above, informed me that the drops were just temporary "market corrections." Looking back at Figure 1.1, that was sure one big correction.

So, why did the investment company I was using, and every other brokerage house I can think of, not tell their customers the obvious truth? The reason is that most financial advisors make their money from the total funds that they are "managing," not from how much money they make for you. When you really think about it, doesn't that sound ridiculous? Their only incentive is to convince you, by any means possible, to keep your money with them for as long as possible.

Did you know that less than 10 percent of *fund managers* ("experts" who buy, sell, and manage a mutual fund's portfolio) actually do better than a plain vanilla *index fund* (a fund that follows an index, such as the Dow Jones—so if the Dow goes up 10 percent, the fund's price does, too). These managers have MBAs from Ivy League universities, receive six- to seven-digit incomes and bonuses, and cannot even beat the market! (And where do you think they're getting their huge paychecks from?)

fund manager the individual responsible for making portfolio decisions for a mutual fund, pension fund, or insurance fund.

index fund a passively managed mutual fund that tries to mirror the performance of a specific index, such as the Standard & Poor's 500. Since portfolio decisions are automatic and transactions are infrequent, expenses tend to be lower than those of actively managed funds.

At the very least, if you decide my emerging markets strategy is too risky for you, take control of your own portfolio and invest in index funds and *blue chips* (IBM, Microsoft, Mobil, etc.) You can buy these funds and stocks using the simple techniques that are discussed later.

blue chip stock of a large, national company with a solid record of stable earnings and/or dividend growth and a reputation for high-quality management and/or products. More generally, anything of very high quality.

If your mother did not tell you, let me: DON'T TRUST ANYONE WITH YOUR MONEY!

One of my friends, a physician, was telling me how much his salary was and how much more he would make if he hired another doctor to work out of his office. When I asked him how his investments were doing, he did not have too much information on them—his financial advisor handled them—but he did recall that his returns were not that great. Imagine: He spends so much time concerned about making more money as a physician but spends no time on his own investments. Can you believe that he is paying someone to gamble with his money—someone who has a 90 percent chance of not even beating an index fund.

Regardless of your job or profession, we must all become our own part-time financial experts (unless, of course, you really do not care about making money). It is imperative that we take the necessary time to learn the basics of investing and, at the very least, learn how to buy and sell simple index funds over the Internet. Look at it as a part-time job.

YOU CAN MAKE A LOT OF MONEY

I hope the last section motivated you to take over the reins of your financial future. Now, however, I would like to get back to the benefits of investing in emerging market funds. The primary incentive is that you can make a lot of money. And that is a pretty good benefit, I must say. I believe that you can make a fortune investing in emerging markets, compared with U.S. stocks. Let us look at Figure 1.4 so I can show you why.

The figure depicts one of my favorite stocks, the Indonesia Fund. This stock is an index fund that closely follows the Jakarta Stock Exchange. Take a close look at the figure and see if you can figure out why this would be a good medium- to long-term investment for the new millennium.

Now let us look at a U.S. index fund, shown in Figure 1.5. Because the WEBS index fund family has been around for only a few years, the figure does not go back as far as the Indonesia Fund. But the differences are obvious. Indonesia is at a 10-year low, and the United States is at an all-time high.

Now, no one knows where markets will go—they could go up or down or all over the place. But one thing I know: The United States surely has a lot of room to fall and make a huge splash. In contrast, In-

FIGURE 1.4 Indonesia Fund, 1990 to 2000.

donesia and most emerging markets are pretty much bottomed out; they have a lot of room to go up.

All of my money will be in emerging market funds in the coming years, as Asia comes out of its recession. Hey, it does not take a genius to see this (but why hasn't your financial advisor told you about this great news?). Remember, unlike a company, which can go out of business, these countries (and their funds) will always be around. (By the way, wars and natural disasters make for great shopping sprees. Now you can become a cold-hearted vulture like the financial barons.)

For a real-life example and projection into the future, consider a \$10,000 investment in the Indonesia Fund in January of 2001. At that time, the stock price should be at least \$4.25. With a margin loan, which we will discuss later, you can now purchase \$20,000 worth of stock (stocks valued under $4^1/_8$ are not marginable according to Fed regulations). Now you own around 4,700 shares of IF (Indonesia Fund's symbol). Suppose, in a few months, the price rises to \$6, your stock is worth \$28,200 (4,700 shares times \$6 per share). After paying back your loan, you've made \$8,200—*an 82 percent return in only a few months*!

FIGURE 1.5 WEBS Index Fund U.S., 1996 to 2000.

I am not making this stuff up! I do it every day. And remember, the markets are (and will be even in early 2001) bottomed out, so the risk is very limited. Of course you will want to keep buying up more shares with your profits and continue to take out additional margin loans and invest that money as well. This leveraging effect has amazing results.

(A reminder: There is a big down side to leveraging—when markets are high, and one is heavily leveraged with margin loans, leveraging can work against you in a big way. But again, that is why this is a unique and ideal time in global stock market history: Asian and other emerging countries have hit bottom; and U.S. interest rates are rising again—so you always will know the limits of drops.)

My prediction is that the Indonesia Fund will hit $10 a share—at least—by the end of the year 2001. Is that a good enough reason for you to invest in emerging markets?

Chapter 2

The Players: The Emerging Market Index Funds

WHAT IS A FUND, ANYWAY?

When I mention that I invest in emerging or international markets, many people think that I must be shipping my money abroad and entrusting banana republic banks with my hard-earned savings; or, that I fly out to the bush in a pontoon plane, continue on through a thick jungle in a Land Rover, and hand over large amounts of money to an antigovernment guerrilla force. Sounds risky to me too! I don't think I could sleep at night if all of my money were held out of the United States like that.

But I invest in international markets with stocks traded on American stock exchanges—either the NYSE (New York Stock Exchange) or Nasdaq (National Association of Security Dealers). With my money in the hands of the world's last superpower, it is relatively safe, I believe.

When I say I invest in stocks, I am actually investing in closed-end funds traded on the stock exchanges just mentioned. They are traded like any other stock, such as IBM or Mobil. So why are they funds? How can you invest in a foreign country with a fund or stock traded on a U.S. exchange? All good questions. Let us start with the definition of a "fund" first.

By fund, I'm referring to a mutual fund. A mutual fund is a pool of money, controlled and managed by a company. Often a large investment company runs many mutual funds, each with its own fund management team, consisting of fund management experts, analysts, and specialists. Each mutual fund has a specific specialty, whether it be technology companies, NYSE Blue Chip companies, or health-related companies. In my case, I deal in funds that specialize in single, developing countries.

A fund's management team monitors the market, searching for good companies to invest in and good opportunities to sell current holdings. In the case of an emerging market fund, such as a China fund, for example, the fund will purchase shares in Chinese companies over the Hong Kong Stock Exchange or over China's two stock exchanges, Shanghai or Shenzen. (Some funds even may specialize in American companies with major international operations in developing countries.)

So where do the funds get their investment *capital*? From you and me. We purchase shares of their fund, and they put our money into a pool, or fund, and invest it according to their *charter*.

capital cash or goods used to generate income.

charter a document, filed with a U.S. state by a corporation's founders, describing the purpose, place of business, and other details of a corporation.

The concept of a fund is based on the premise that there are indeed people out there who are financial experts and specialists, and we could use their knowledge and expertise with our investments. Although I criticized financial advisors in Chapter 1, by no means do I mean that no one in the financial industry should be trusted. I have no desire to purchase individual shares of stock of foreign companies over international stock exchanges—doing so would be tremendously time consuming, costly, and risky.

Many mutual fund companies send specialists out to these emerging countries to visit the management teams of the companies they are considering investing in. When I worked for Standard Chartered Bank in Hong Kong, one of my tasks was to design programs for the biyearly visits of investment company analysts. A few times a year, major investment companies would send a representative or two to out to Hong Kong to meet with the companies they have large holdings with and with companies they are considering investing in. We would host a group of representatives from 10 or so companies, introducing them to each division head. Over a two-day period, each division head would give them a tour of their areas, and a slick presentation of their division's performance and future strategy. If the investors liked what they saw, they would invest in our bank.

Other fund companies simply purchase shares of a representative number of companies traded on a particular stock exchange. These are index funds. There are index funds for most American and international exchanges. Index funds are designed to follow the price changes of the index. So, if the Dow Jones Industrial Average goes up 1.5 percent on a particular day, a Dow Jones index fund would increase by the same amount.

This book is about investing in index funds of emerging markets, or funds that closely mimic the indexes of these exchanges. Thus, if the Hong Kong Hang Seng Index rises by 1.5 percent, your Hong Kong index fund would rise by about the same amount.

There are also two different types of funds: closed end and open end. This is an important point, because there's a major difference between the two. (This book concentrates on closed-end funds, if you recall.) An open-end fund is one that does not have a set amount of *shares*. For example, a fund may start out issuing 100,000 shares. Each share is worth a certain amount of money, depending on the value of the fund's portfolio. Once the 100,000 shares are purchased, the fund managers can issue additional shares if they feel there are good invest-

> **share** certificate representing one unit of ownership in a corporation, mutual fund, or limited partnership.

ment opportunities with the additional funds they receive. For example, as a fund manager, I may see a number of new investment opportunities, but the money from the 100,000 shares is already fully invested. Then I could elect to issues additional shares—say 25,000—and invest it in these promising companies.

The value of a share of an open-end fund goes up and down with the overall value of the holdings in the *portfolio*.

> **portfolio** a collection of investments all owned by the same individual or organization.

There is a major drawback to open-end funds, by the way. Say the market has taken a nosedive, and a great number of people who own shares of the fund wish to sell out. Where does the fund get the money to pay these folks as they sell their shares? The fund has to start selling off an equal value of its portfolio, and the prime stock is sold first. In a panic-stricken market, fund managers may have to sell their portfolio off at ridiculously low prices. Basically, the fund may be stuck with a lackluster group of companies in its portfolio, which affects the future value of the fund for those who still own shares.

Another big drawback to open-end mutual funds is that fund management companies usually charge high fees to purchase, maintain, and sell holdings with them. When I invested in open-ended funds while living in Asia, I paid 3 to 5 percent of my investment just to purchase shares plus a 1 to 3 percent management fee each year. So, even though I might be making a 10 to 20 percent return each month, every time I would sell, my profit would decrease significantly.

Closed-end funds, on the other hand, have a fixed number of shares; once the original shares are sold, no additional shares will be created. For example, First Australia Fund (IAF) has 15,894,000 outstanding shares. Someone—an individual investor or investment company—owns each and every one of these shares. The shares are traded as stock on the Nasdaq stock exchange. When a person wishes to sell shares, Nasdaq offers them to potential buyers. When the seller's *ask* price matches with a buyer's *bid* price, the stock is transferred. Unlike the open-end fund, additional shares will not be created when demand for the fund increases; the stock price will simply increase to reflect the greater demand.

ask the lowest price that any investor or dealer has declared that he or she will sell a given security or commodity for. For over-the-counter stocks, the ask is the best quoted price at which a market maker is willing to sell a stock. For mutual funds, the ask is the net asset value plus any sales charges. Also called asked price, asking price, or offering price.

bid the highest price any buyer is willing to pay for a given security at a given time; also called bid price.

That is why I am so excited trading in the stocks that I do: I invest in emerging markets by purchasing stocks that I have become very familiar and comfortable with, over safe American stock exchanges. I know that the price I buy and sell stock at are fair market prices.

THE COUNTRY FUNDS

The following section presents the emerging markets that I follow; it provides discussion and brief analysis of the countries themselves and information on their index funds. There is a lot of information here, including political and economic information. I feel that it is important that we understand where our money is going. My investment strategies are not based solely on chart analysis but also on a detailed presentation of country fundamentals. For example, as you know, I have lived and traveled throughout Asia. I believe strongly in the long-term future of these economies. On the other hand, I am not so confident about the medium- and long-term *fundamentals* of Russia. Both China and Russia are former communist states. However, I feel that the Chinese government is on the right path to market reform. From my experience, the Chinese culture itself is based on market capitalism. Russia, on the other hand, seems to be having a more difficult transition moving from a communist to free market economy. As you read the country briefs, you will get a feel for which countries have good short-, medium-, and long-term investment potential. If there were an earthquake in Turkey, for example, although you may not feel that Turkey was a good long-term bet, the earthquake may present a good short-term investment opportunity. Catastrophic events often lead to significant short-term drops in the country's stock market, with a rebound shortly thereafter, thus providing an ideal short-term opportunity. If the country in question had a bright outlook overall, according to one's analysis, this could be an ideal time to buy for the long term as well.

fundamentals the basics, as of a business.

The information presented was gathered from the following sources: the Central Intelligence Agency, the Bureau of Labor Statistics (Department of Labor), the Bureau of the Census (Department of Commerce), and various other public sources.

Figure 2.1 is a list of the country funds I follow, categorized by re-

Asia	***Funds***
Australia	EWA, IAF
China/Hong Kong	CHN, EWH, GCH, TCH
India	IFN, IIF, JFI
Indonesia	IF
Japan	EWJ, JEQ
Korea	KEF, KF
Malaysia	EWM, MF
Pakistan	PKF
Philippines	FPF
Singapore	EWS, SGF
Taiwan	TWN, TYW
Thailand	TC, TTF
Vietnam	TVF
South America	***Funds***
Argentina	AF
Brazil	BZF, BZL
Chile	CH
Mexico	EWW, MXF
Africa/Mideast	***Funds***
Israel	ISL
South Africa	AFF, SOA
Europe	***Funds***
Portugal	PGF
Russia	RNE, TRF
Spain	EWP, SNF
Turkey	TKF

FIGURE 2.1 Fund list by region and country.

gion. Many international open- and closed-end funds are available, but these are the primary single country emerging market funds.

Chapter 3 discusses stock analysis software and various tools for basic stock analysis. I feel it is important to first understand *why* you should invest in emerging markets (from Chapter 1), then learn *what* you'll be investing in, before learning *when* and *how* to invest.

THE ASIAN MARKETS

FIGURE 2.2

AUSTRALIA

FIGURE 2.3

Country Brief

Personal Thoughts: I love a good 18-ounce steak at the Outback, but I'm not a frequent investor in the Australian funds. Australia, often considered part of Asia, is actually more like a developed European country: not enough volatility for my liking, mate!

Area: 7,686,850 square kilometers (slightly smaller than the United States)

Population: 18,613,087

Life Expectancy: 79.89 years

Ethnic Groups: Caucasian 92%; Asian 7%; aboriginal and other 1%

Religions: Anglican 26.1%; Roman Catholic 26%; other Christian 24.3%; non-Christian 11%

Languages: English, native languages

Literacy: Total population: 100%

Government Type: Democratic, federal-state system recognizing the British monarch as sovereign

Economy Overview: Australia has a prosperous Western-style capitalist economy, with a per-capita gross domestic product (GDP) at the level of the highly industrialized West European countries. Rich in natural resources, Australia is a major exporter of agricultural products, minerals, metals, and fossil fuels. Commodities account for 57 percent of the value of total exports, so that a downturn in world commodity prices can have a big impact on the economy. Australia has suffered from the low growth and high unemployment characterizing the member countries of the Organization for Economic Cooperation and Development (OECD) in the early 1990s, but the economy has expanded at reasonably steady rates in recent years. Canberra's emphasis on reforms is a key factor behind the economy's resilience to the regional crisis and its stronger-than-expected growth rate that reached 4.5 percent in 1999.

GDP/Real Growth Rate: $394 billion/4.5%

GDP—Per Capita: $21,400

GDP by Sector: Agriculture: 4%; industry: 31%; services: 65%

Inflation Rate: 1%

Labor Force: Total: 9.2 million

Unemployment Rate: 8.4%

Exports/Imports: $68 billion/$67 billion

Debt—External: $150 billion

Military Expenditures/% of GDP: $6.9 billion/1.9%

Australia's Index Funds: EWA and IAF

First Australia Fund (IAF) (Nasdaq)

Chart Period: 14 years

Period High: $14.5 *Period Low:* $5.12

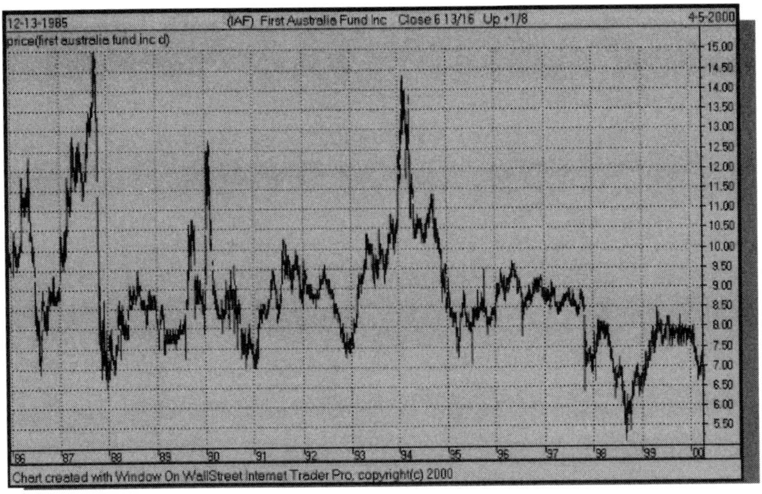

FIGURE 2.4 First Australia Fund (IAF), 1986 to 2000.

Total Shares Outstanding: 15,894,000

Market Capitalization: $ 108,000,000

Fund Management: First Australia Fund, Inc., Gateway Center Three, 101 Mulberry Street, Newark, New Jersey 07102-4077, 800-632-3277

WEBS Australia (EWA) (Nasdaq)

Chart Period: 3 years

Period High: $11.62 *Period Low:* $7.38

Total Shares Outstanding: 13,003,000

Market Capitalization: $130,030,000

Fund Management: WEBS Index Fund, Inc., 400 Bellevue Parkway, Wilmington, Delaware 19809, 800-810-9327

CHINA

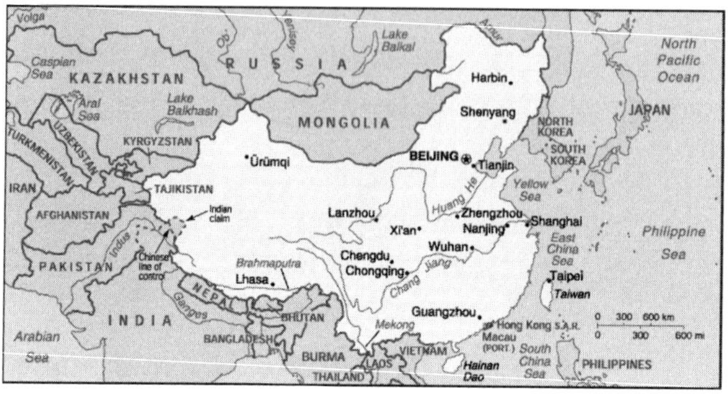

FIGURE 2.5

Country Brief

Personal Thoughts: China and Hong Kong are personal favorites of mine—and not just because I lived there. The Chinese people are very, very money oriented—and I mean that in a good way. I have 100% confidence in China for the next 10 to 20 years, both politically and economically.

Area: Total: 9,596,960 square kilometers (slightly smaller than the United States)

Population: 1,236,914,658

Life Expectancy at Birth: 69.59 years

Ethnic Groups: Han Chinese 91.9%; Zhuang, Uygur, Hui, Yi, Tibetan, Miao, Manchu, Mongol, Buyi, Korean, and other nationalities 8.1%

Religions: Daoism (Taoism), Buddhism, Muslim 2–3%; Christian 1% (est.). Note: Officially atheist but traditionally pragmatic and eclectic.

Languages: Standard Chinese or Mandarin (Putonghua, based on the Beijing dialect), Yue (Cantonese), Wu (Shanghaiese), Minbei

(Fuzhou), Minnan (Hokkien-Taiwanese), Xiang, Gan, Hakka dialects, minority languages

Literacy: 81.5%

Government Type: Communist state

Economy Overview: Since late 1978 the Chinese leadership has been trying to move the economy from a sluggish Soviet-style centrally planned economy to a more market-oriented economy but still within a rigid political framework of Communist Party control. To this end the authorities switched to a system of household responsibility in agriculture in place of the old collectivization, increased the authority of local officials and plant managers in industry, permitted a wide variety of small-scale enterprise in services and light manufacturing, and opened the economy to increased foreign trade and investment. The result has been a quadrupling of GDP since 1978. On the darker side, the leadership often has experienced in its hybrid system the worst results of socialism (bureaucracy, lassitude, corruption) and of capitalism (windfall gains and stepped-up inflation). Beijing thus has periodically backtracked, tightening central controls at intervals. In late 1993 China's leadership approved additional long-term reforms aimed at giving still more play to market-oriented institutions and at strengthening the center's control over the financial system; state enterprises would continue to dominate many key industries in what was now termed "a socialist market economy." The next few years may witness increasing tensions between a highly centralized political system and an increasingly decentralized economic system. Economic growth probably will slow to more moderate levels in 2000–2001.

GDP/Real Growth Rate: $4.25 trillion/8.8%

GDP—Per Capita: $3,600

GDP by Sector: Agriculture: 20%; industry: 49%; services: 31% (1996 est.)

Inflation Rate: 0.8%

Labor Force: 623.9 million

Unemployment Rate: Officially 3% in urban areas; probably 8 to 10%.

Exports/Imports: $182.7 billion/$142.4 billion

Debt—External: $159 billion

China's Index Funds

As most of the primary holdings of "China" funds are in companies traded over the Hong Kong exchange, China's index funds are covered under Hong Kong's discussion.

HONG KONG

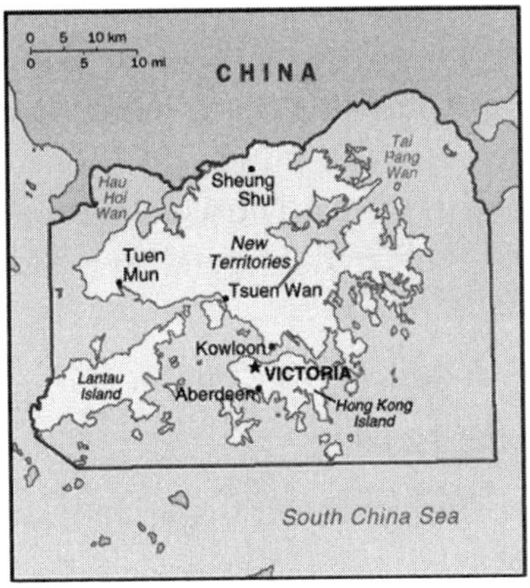

FIGURE 2.6

Country Brief

Personal Thoughts: Step off the plane into Hong Kong's airport and you will feel an immediate rush of energy—people pushing and shoving and rushing about. Hong Kong is the fastest-paced city in the world—it beats New York City by far. Strip Hong Kong of its political freedom, and the stock market still booms.

Area: 1,092 square kilometers (six times the size of Washington, D.C.)

Population: 6,706,965

Life Expectancy at Birth: 78.81 years

Ethnic Groups: Chinese 95%, other 5%

Religions: Eclectic mixture of local religions 90%; Christian 10%

Languages: Chinese (Cantonese), English

Literacy: 92.2%

Government Type: Special administrative region of China

Overview: Hong Kong has a bustling free market economy highly dependent on international trade. Natural resources are limited, and food and raw materials must be imported.

A shortage of labor continues to put upward pressure on prices and the cost of living. Even before Hong Kong reverted to Chinese administration on July 1, 1997 it had extensive trade and investment ties with China. The widespread Asian economic difficulties in 1998 hit this trade-dependent economy quite hard, with GDP down 5%.

GDP/Real Growth Rate: $175.2 billion/5%

GDP—Per Capita: $26,800

GDP by Sector: Agriculture: 0.1%; industry: 16.1%; services: 83.8% (1996 est.)

Inflation Rate: 2.9%

Labor Force: 3.183 million

Unemployment Rate: 5.5%

Exports/Imports: $180.7 billion/$198.6 billion

Debt—External: None

Military Expenditures: NA

Hong Kong/China's Index Funds: CHN, EWH, GCH, TCH

The China Fund, Inc. (CHN) (NYSE)

Chart Period: 7 years

Period High: $27.5 *Period Low:* $4.93

Total Shares Outstanding: 10,844,937

Market Capitalization: $106,000,000

Fund Management: The China Fund, Inc. (State Street Bank & Trust, P.O. Box 9110, North Quincy, Massachusetts 02171, 212-808-0500)

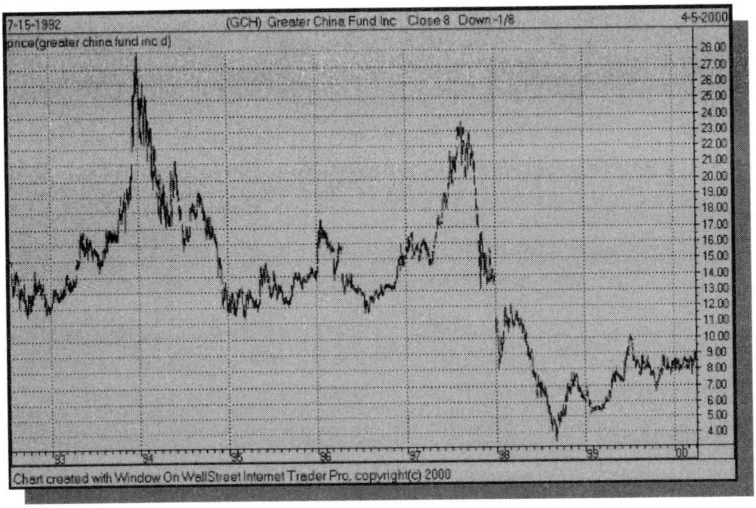

FIGURE 2.7 Greater China Fund (GCH), 1992 to 2000.

Hong Kong WEBS Index Series (EWH) (Nasdaq)

Chart Period: 3.5 years

Period High: $18 *Period Low:* $5.31

Total Shares Outstanding: 13,003,000

Market Capitalization: $169,000,000

Fund Management: WEBS Index Fund, Inc. (400 Bellevue Parkway, Wilmington, Delaware 19809, 800-810-9327)

The Greater China Fund, Inc. (GCH) (NYSE)

Chart Period: 7 years

Period High: $27.50 *Period Low:* $3.50

Total Shares Outstanding: 12,593,048

Market Capitalization: $101,000,000

Fund Management: The Greater China Fund, Inc. (Mitchell Hutchins Asset Management, 1285 Avenue of the Americas, 16th Floor, New York, New York 10019)

Templeton China World Fund, Inc. (TCH) (NYSE)

Chart Period: 7 years

Period High: $20.00 *Period Low:* $4.25

Total Shares Outstanding: 20,384,000

Market Capitalization: $153,000,000

Fund Management: Templeton China World Fund, Inc. (Broward Financial Center, 500 E. Broward Boulevard, Suite 2100, Ft. Lauderdale, Florida 33394, 305-527-7500)

INDIA

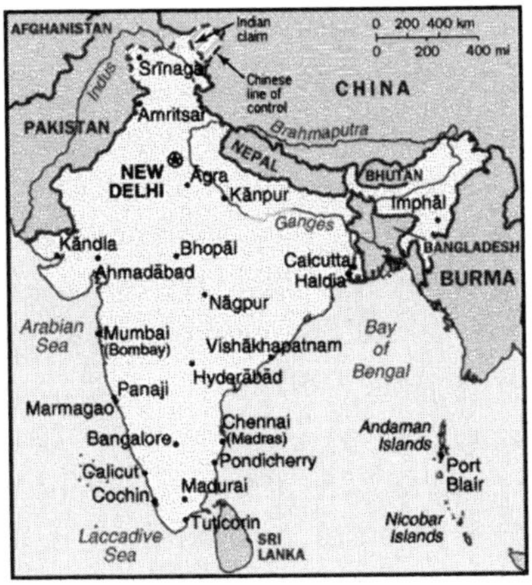

FIGURE 2.8

Country Brief

Personal Thoughts: India was the first country I ever made a fortune in. Even though India has low literacy and low per-capita GDP and ethnic strife, it is still one of my favorite countries to invest in and has never failed to make money for me.

Area: 3,287,590 square kilometers (slightly more than one third the size of the United States)

Population: 984,003,683

Life Expectancy at Birth: 62.9 years

Ethnic Groups: Indo-Aryan 72%; Dravidian 25%; Mongoloid and other 3%

Religions: Hindu 80%; Muslim 14%; Christian 2.4%; Sikh 2%; Buddhist 0.7%; Jain 0.5%; other 0.4%

Languages: English enjoys associate status but is the most important language for national, political, and commercial communication.

Hindi is the national language and primary tongue of 30% of the people.

Literacy: 52%

Government Type: Federal republic

Economy Overview: India's economy encompasses traditional village farming, modern agriculture, handicrafts, a wide range of modern industries, and a multitude of support services. In India, 67 percent of the labor force of nearly 400 million work in agriculture, which contributes 30 percent of the country's GDP. Production, trade, and investment reforms since 1991 have provided new opportunities for Indian businesspeople and an estimated 300 million middle-class consumers. The Indian government needs to restore the early momentum of reform, especially by continuing reductions in the extensive remaining government regulations. Moreover, economic policy changes have not yet significantly increased jobs or reduced the risk that international financial strains will re-emerge within the next few years. Nearly 40 percent of the Indian population remains too poor to afford an adequate diet. Inflation will remain a worrisome problem.

GDP/Real Growth Rate: $1.534 trillion/5%

GDP—Per Capita: $1,600

GDP by Sector: Agriculture: 30%; industry: 28%; services: 42% (1996 est.)

Inflation Rate: 14%

Labor Force: 390 million

Unemployment Rate: NA

Exports/Imports: $33.9 billion/$39.7 billion

Debt—External: $90.7 billion

Military Expenditures/% of GDP: $10 billion/2.7%

India's Index Funds: IFN, IIF, JFI

The India Fund, Inc. (IFN) (NYSE)

Chart Period: 6 years

Period High: $21.5 *Period Low:* $5.19

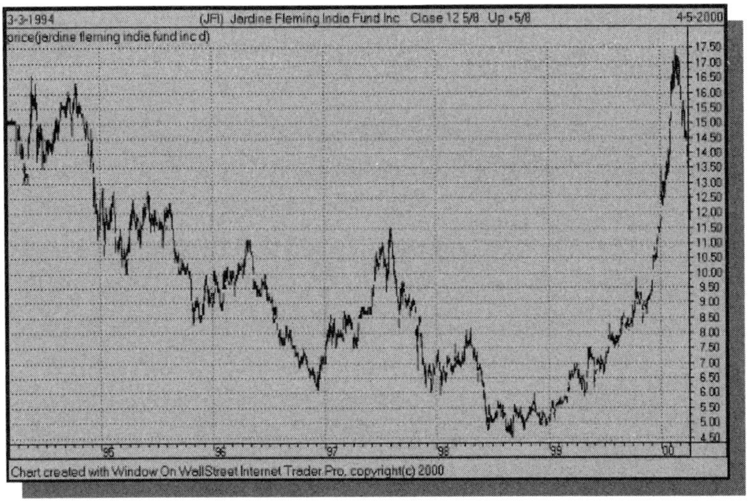

FIGURE 2.9 Jardine Fleming India Fund (JFI), 1994 to 2000.

Total Shares Outstanding: 34,007,133

Market Capitalization: $510,000,000

Fund Management: The India Fund (Oppenheimer Tower, 200 Liberty Street, 38th Floor, New York, New York 10281)

Morgan Stanley India Investment Fund, Inc. (IIF) (NYSE)

Chart Period: 6 years

Period High: $18.75 *Period Low:* $5.75

Total Shares Outstanding: 35,000,000

Market Capitalization: $451,000,000

Fund Management: Morgan Stanley Dean Witter India Investment Fund, Inc. (American Stock Transfer and Trust Company, 40 Wall Street, New York, New York 10005)

Jardine Fleming India Fund, Inc. (JFI) (NYSE)

Chart Period: 6 years

Period High: $17.50 *Period Low:* $4.50

Total Shares Outstanding: 11,307,169

Market Capitalization: $143,000,000

Fund Management: Jardine Fleming India Fund, Inc. (Mitchell Hutchins Asset Management, 1285 Avenue of the Americas, New York, New York 10019)

INDONESIA

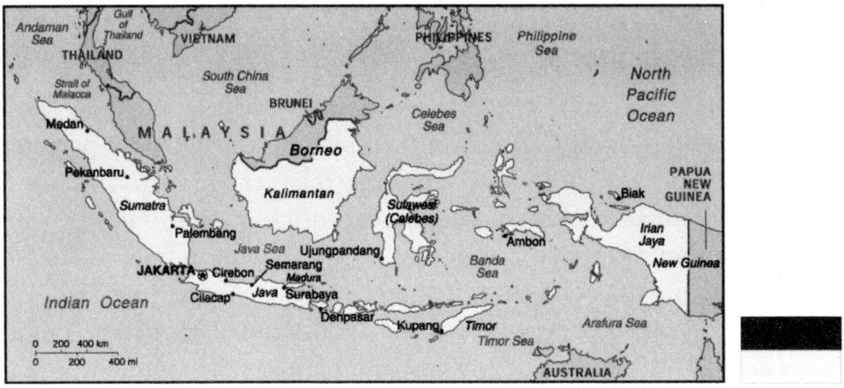

FIGURE 2.10

Country Brief

Personal Thoughts: Without a doubt, Indonesia and Malaysia are my two favorite countries to invest in. Both countries recently have had major political strife, but they will work through these issues in the next few years. Both countries have a strict Muslim culture and strong work ethics—and, just as important, predictably volatile stock markets.

Area: 1,919,440 square kilometers (slightly less than three times the size of Texas)

Population: 212,941,810

Life Expectancy at Birth: 62.49 years

Ethnic Groups: Javanese 45%; Sundanese 14%; Madurese 7.5%; coastal Malays 7.5%; other 26%

Religions: Muslim 87%; Protestant 6%; Roman Catholic 3%; Hindu 2%; Buddhist 1%; other 1% (1985)

Languages: Bahasa Indonesia (official, modified form of Malay),

English, Dutch, local dialects, the most widely spoken of which is Javanese

Literacy: 83.8%

Government Type: Republic

Economy Overview: The collapse of the rupiah in late 1997 and early 1998 caused GDP to contract by an estimated 13.7 percent in 1998 because of Indonesian firms' reliance on short-term dollar-denominated debt and high levels of nonperforming loans in the banking sector. The Indonesian government initially wavered on meeting the conditions it agreed to in exchange for a $42 billion assistance package from the International Monetary Fund (IMF), contributing to further loss of investor confidence and outflows of capital. Riots that in many cases targeted ethnic Chinese business owners also set back chances that Indonesia would quickly stabilize its financial crisis and contributed to President Soeharto's resignation on May 21, 1998. His successor, B.J. Habibie, improved cooperation with the IMF. The money supply—which expanded rapidly early in the year to prop up banks hit by deposit runs—was tightened within a few months and by October inflation—which reached a 77 percent annual rate—was significantly dampened. The government also announced a bank recapitalization program in late 1998, but by early 1999 the plan faced growing challenges over its reliance on public funds. Doubts about whether the program is adequate underlie forecasts of continued—although much less severe—GDP contraction for 1999. Signs of spreading unrest and sectarian violence and concern about increased social instability around the June 7, 1999, national election have also contributed to pessimism about the economy, particularly because foreign investors remain reluctant to begin to increase capital inflows again. The next government will face the challenge of establishing a macroeconomic policy framework that addresses long-standing grievances and inequities underlying much of the current unrest without hampering an economic recovery.

GDP/Real Growth Rate: $602 billion/-13.7%

GDP—Per Capita: $2,830

GDP by Sector: Agriculture: 16%; industry: 43%; services: 41% (1996)

Inflation Rate: 77%

Labor Force: 87 million

Unemployment Rate: 15–20%

Exports/Imports: $49 billion/$24 billion

Debt—External: $136 billion

Military Expenditures/% of GDP: $959 million/1%

Indonesia's Index Fund: IF

The Indonesia Fund, Inc. (IF) (NYSE)

Chart Period: 10 years

Period High: $23.00 *Period Low:* $2.25

FIGURE 2.11 Indonesia Fund (IF), 1990 to 2000.

Total Shares Outstanding: 4,608,989

Market Capitalization: $19,000,000

Fund Management: Credit Suisse Asset Management (153 E. 53rd Street, New York, New York 10022)

JAPAN

FIGURE 2.12

Country Brief

Personal Thoughts: Boring! Great people, wonderful culture, but totally unpredictable economy. In the early 1980s, Japan was to be the next superpower. I don't know where it has been or what it has been up to since.

Area: 377,835 square kilometers (slightly smaller than California)

Population: 125,931,533

Life Expectancy at Birth: 80 years

Ethnic Groups: Japanese 99.4%; other 0.6% (mostly Korean)

Religions: Observe both Shinto and Buddhist 84%, other 16% (including Christian 0.7%)

Languages: Japanese

Literacy: 99%

Government Type: Constitutional monarchy

Economy Overview: Government-industry cooperation, a strong work ethic, mastery of high technology, and a comparatively small defense allocation (roughly 1% of gross domestic product) have helped Japan advance with extraordinary rapidity to the rank of second most powerful economy in the world. One notable characteristic of the economy is that manufacturers, suppliers, and distributors work together in closely knit groups called *keiretsu*. A second basic feature has been the guarantee of lifetime employment for a substantial portion of the urban labor force; this guarantee has been eroding recently. Industry, the most important sector of the economy, depends heavily on imported raw materials and fuels. The much smaller agricultural sector is highly subsidized and protected, with crop yields among the highest in the world. Usually self-sufficient in rice, Japan must import about 50% of its requirements of other grain and fodder crops. Growth slowed markedly from 1992 to 1995 largely because of the aftereffects of overinvestment during the late 1980s and contradictory domestic policies intended to wring speculative excesses from the stock and real estate markets. In 1997–1998 Japan experienced a wrenching recession, centered on financial difficulties in the banking system and real estate markets and exacerbated by rigid corporate structures and labor markets. In early 1999 output started to stabilize as emergency government spending began to take hold. The crowding of habitable land area and the aging of the population are two major long-run problems.

GDP/Real Growth Rate: $3.08 trillion/–2.6%

GDP—Per Capita: $24,500

GDP by Sector: Agriculture: 2%; industry: 41.5%; services: 56.5%

Inflation Rate: 0.9%

Labor Force: 67.23 million

Unemployment Rate: 4.4%

Exports/Imports: $421 billion/$339 billion

Debt—External: NA

Military Expenditures/% of GDP: $48.5 billion/1%

Japan's Index Funds: EWJ and JEQ

Japan WEBS Index Series (EWJ) (Nasdaq)

Chart Period: 4 years

Period High: $16.50 *Period Low:* $7.50

Total Shares Outstanding: 13,003,000

Market Capitalization: $207,000,000

Fund Management: WEBS Index Fund, Inc. (400 Bellevue Parkway, Wilmington, Delaware 19809, 800-810-9327)

FIGURE 2.13 Japan Equity Fund (JEQ), 1992 to 2000.

The Japan Equity Fund, Inc. (JEQ) (NYSE)

Chart Period: 8 years

Period High: $18.00 *Period Low:* $5.38

Total Shares Outstanding: 11,000,000

Market Capitalization: $89,000,000

Fund Management: Daiwa Securities Trust Company (One Evertrust Plaza, Jersey City, New Jersey 07302)

KOREA

FIGURE 2.14

Country Brief

Personal Thoughts: Not as volatile as Indonesia and Malaysia, but Korea still has good long-term investment potential. I often buy both of Korea's index funds.

Area: 98,480 square kilometers (slightly larger than Indiana)

Population: 46,416,796

Life Expectancy at Birth: 73.95 years

Ethnic Groups: Homogeneous (except for about 20,000 Chinese)

Religions: Christianity 49%; Buddhism 47%; Confucianism 3%; pervasive folk religion (Shamanism), Chondogyo (Religion of the Heavenly Way), and other 1%

Languages: Korean; English widely taught in junior high and high school

Literacy: 98%

Government Type: Republic

Economy Overview: As one of the Four Dragons of East Asia, South Korea has achieved an incredible record of growth. Three decades ago its GDP per capita was comparable with levels in the poorer countries of Africa and Asia. Today its GDP per capita is eight times India's, 15 times North Korea's, and matches the lesser economies of the European Union. This success was achieved by a system of close government ties with business, including directed credit, import restrictions, sponsorship of specific industries, and a strong labor effort. The Asian financial crisis of 1997–1998 exposed certain long-standing weaknesses in South Korea's development model, including high debt/equity ratios, massive foreign borrowing, and an undisciplined financial sector. As of December 1998, the first tentative signs of a rebound in the economy emerged, and most forecasters expect GDP growth to turn positive at least in the second half of 1999. Seoul also has made a positive start on a program to get the country's largest business groups to swap subsidiaries to promote specialization, and the administration has directed many of the midsize conglomerates into debt-workout programs with creditor banks. Challenges for the future include cutting redundant staff, which reaches 20 to 30 percent at most firms, and maintaining the impetus for structural reform.

GDP/Real Growth Rate: $584 billion/–6%

GDP—Per Capita: $13,700

GDP by Sector: Agriculture: 8%; industry: 45%; services: 47%

Inflation Rate: 7.5%

Labor Force: 20 million

Unemployment Rate: 7.9%

Exports/Imports: \$133 billion/\$94 billion

Debt—External: \$154 billion

Military Expenditures/% of GDP: \$9.9 billion/3.3%

Korea's Index Funds: KEF and KF

Korea Equity Fund, Inc. (KEF) (NYSE)

Chart Period: 6 years

Period High: \$15.00 *Period Low:* \$1.88

Total Shares Outstanding: 8,400,000

Market Capitalization: \$32,000,000

Fund Management: Korea Equity Fund, Inc. (180 Maiden Lane, New York, New York 10038-4936, 800-833-0018)

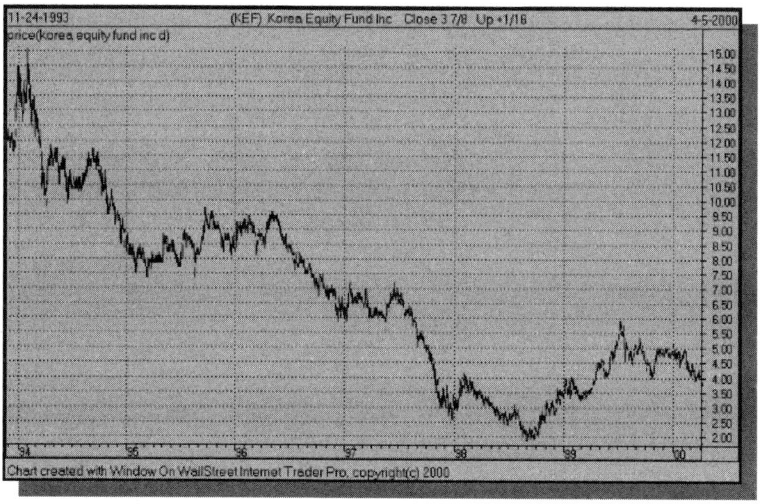

FIGURE 2.15 Korea Equity Fund (KEF), 1994 to 2000.

The Korea Fund, Inc. (KF) (NYSE)

Chart Period: 16 years

Period High: $42.50 *Period Low:* $4.25

Total Shares Outstanding: 49,999,999

Market Capitalization: $693,750,000

Fund Management: The Korea Fund, Inc. (c/o Scudder Stevens & Clark, Inc., 345 Park Avenue, New York, New York 10154, 617-330-5464)

MALAYSIA

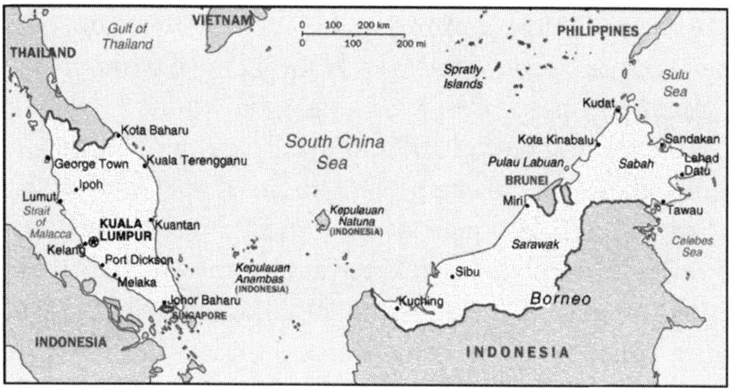

FIGURE 2.16

Country Brief

Personal Thoughts: Wonderful country, wonderful investment! I enjoyed night diving with giant turtles off of Tioman Island, and I enjoy buying the Malaysia Fund. Indonesia and Malaysia will be major pieces of my portfolio for the long term.

Area: 329,750 square kilometers (slightly larger than New Mexico)

Population: 20,932,901

Life Expectancy at Birth: 70.36 years

Ethnic Groups: Malay and other indigenous 58%; Chinese 26%; Indian 7%; others 9%

Religions: Islam, Buddhism, Taoism, Hinduism, Christianity, Sikhism, and Shamanism

Languages: Peninsular Malaysia: Malay (official), English, Chinese dialects, Tamil; Sabah: English, Malay, numerous tribal dialects, Chinese (Mandarin and Hakka dialects predominate); Sarawak: English, Malay, Mandarin, numerous tribal languages

Literacy: 83.5%

Government Type: Constitutional monarchy

Economy Overview: After a decade of 8 percent average GDP growth, the Malaysian economy, severely hit by the regional financial crisis, declined 7 percent in 1998. Malaysia will likely remain in recession for the first half of 1999; official statistics continue to show anemic exports, and some private financial analysts forecast a further drop in GDP of 1 percent in 1999. Prime Minister Mahathir has imposed capital controls to protect the local currency while cutting interest rates to stimulate the economy. Kuala Lumpur also announced an expansionary budget for 1999 to combat rising unemployment. Malaysia continues to seek funding from domestic and international sources to help finance its budget deficit and recapitalize its weakened banking sector.

GDP/Real Growth Rate: $227 billion/–7.4%

GDP—Per Capita: $11,100

GDP by Sector: Agriculture: 14%; industry: 45%; services: 41%

Inflation Rate: 5.3%

Labor Force: 8.398 million

Unemployment Rate: 2.6%

Exports/Imports: $74 billion/$59 billion

Debt—External: $39 billion

Military Expenditures/% of GDP: $2.5 billion/2.6%

Malaysia's Index Funds: EWM and MF

Malaysia WEBS Index Series (EWM) (Nasdaq)

Chart Period: 4 years

Period High: $16.00 *Period Low:* $1.63

Total Shares Outstanding: 13,003,000

Market Capitalization: $85,000,000

FIGURE 2.17 Malaysia Fund (MF), 1990 to 2000.

Fund Management: WEBS Index Fund, Inc. (400 Bellevue Parkway, Wilmington, Delaware 19809, 800-810-9327)

The Malaysia Fund, Inc. (MF) (NYSE)

Chart Period: 10 years

Period High: $30.00 *Period Low:* $2.94

Total Shares Outstanding: 9,738,017

Market Capitalization: $60,862,500

Fund Management: Boston Equiserve (Investor Relations Department, P.O. Box 644, Boston, Massachusetts 02102-0644)

PAKISTAN

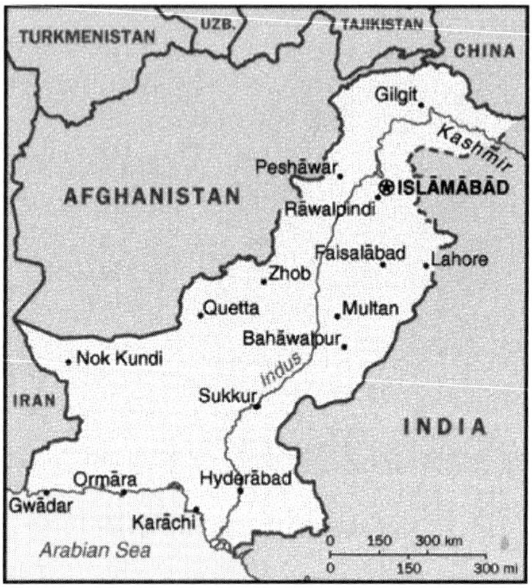

FIGURE 2.18

Country Brief

Personal Thoughts: Pakistan has not been doing much lately—its stock price has been hovering around $3 or so. It is an odd country, with an unpredictable future. I will be watching its index fund closely.

Area: 803,940 square kilometers (slightly less than twice the size of California)

Population: 135,135,195

Life Expectancy at Birth: 59.07 years

Ethnic Groups: Punjabi, Sindhi, Pashtun (Pathan), Baloch, Muhajir (immigrants from India and their descendants)

Religions: Muslim 97% (Sunni 77%, Shi'a 20%); Christian, Hindu, and other 3%

Languages: Punjabi 48%; Sindhi 12%; Siraiki (a Punjabi variant)

10%; Pashtu 8%; Urdu (official) 8%; Balochi 3%; Hindko 2%; Brahui 1%; English (official and lingua franca of Pakistani elite and most government ministries), Burushaski, and other 8%

Literacy: 37.8%

Government Type: Federal republic

Economy Overview: Pakistan continues to suffer through a damaging foreign exchange crisis stemming from years of loose fiscal policies that have exacerbated inflation and allowed public debt to explode. After accruing more than $1.5 billion in debt arrears in the first six months of fiscal year 1998 to 1999, Pakistani officials approached multilateral creditors requesting balance-of-payments relief and structural support. In January 1999 Islamabad received more than $1 billion in loans along with $3 billion in debt relief following the finance minister's pledge to implement an economic reform program to reduce the budget deficit, deepen the financial sector, and broaden the industrial base. Although the economy has shown signs of improvement following implementation of some corrective measures, Prime Minister Sharif historically has failed to implement the tough structural reforms necessary for sustained, longer-term growth. The government also must cope with long-standing economic vulnerabilities: inadequate infrastructure and low levels of literacy.

GDP/Real Growth Rate: $270 billion/5%

GDP—Per Capita: $2,000

GDP by Sector: Agriculture: 24.2%; industry: 26.4% services: 49.4% (1997)

Inflation Rate: 7.8%

Labor Force: 37.8 million

Unemployment Rate: NA

Exports/Imports: $8.2 billion/$11.4 billion

Debt—External: $33 billion

Military Expenditures/% of GDP: $2.48 billion/4.4%

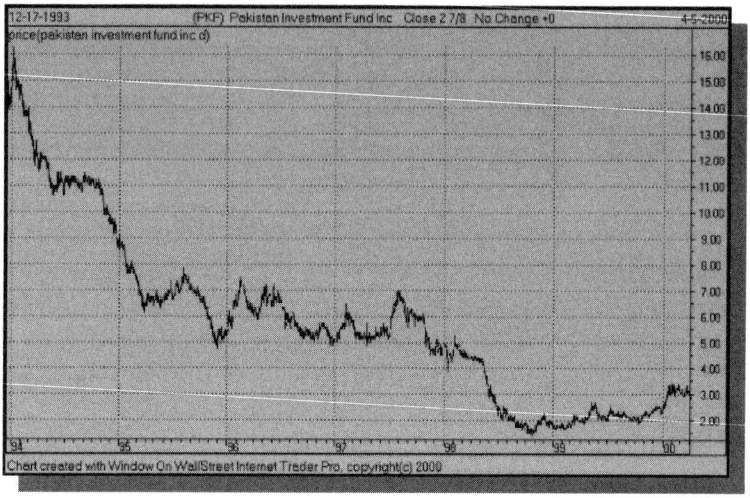

FIGURE 2.19 Pakistan Investment Fund (PKF), 1994 to 2000.

Pakistan's Index Fund: PKF

Pakistan Investment Fund, Inc. (PKF) (NYSE)

Chart Period: 6 years

Period High: $16.00 *Period Low:* $1.44

Total Shares Outstanding: 11,604,793

Market Capitalization: $33,000,000

Fund Management: American Stock Transfer and Trust Company (40 Wall Street, New York, New York 10005)

PHILIPPINES

FIGURE 2.20

Country Brief

Personal Thoughts: Good volatility—good short- to long-term investment potential. The First Philippine Fund is currently a part of my portfolio.

Area: 300,000 square kilometers (slightly larger than Arizona)

Population: 77,725,862

Life Expectancy at Birth: 66.35 years

Ethnic Groups: Christian Malay 91.5%; Muslim Malay 4%; Chinese 1.5%; other 3%

Religions: Roman Catholic 83%; Protestant 9%; Muslim 5%; Buddhist and other 3%

Languages: Filipino (official, based on Tagalog); English (official)

Literacy: 94.6%

Government Type: Republic

Economy Overview: In 1998 the Philippine economy—a mixture of agriculture, light industry, and supporting services—deteriorated as a result of spillover from the Asian financial crisis and poor weather conditions. Growth fell to about –0.5 percent in 1998 from 5 percent in 1997 but is expected to recover to more than 2 percent in 1999. The government has promised to continue its economic reforms to help the Philippines match the pace of development in the newly industrialized countries of East Asia. The strategy includes improving infrastructure, overhauling the tax system to bolster government revenues, and moving toward further deregulation and privatization of the economy.

GDP/Real Growth Rate: $244 billion/–5.1%

GDP—Per Capita: $3,200

GDP by Sector: Agriculture: 22%; industry: 32%; services: 46% (1996 est.)

Inflation Rate: 9.7%

Labor Force: 29.13 million

Unemployment Rate: 9.6%

Exports/Imports: $25 billion/$34 billion

Debt—External: $45.4 billion

Military Expenditures/% of GDP: $995 million/1.5%

Philippines' Index Fund: FPF

The First Philippine Fund, Inc. (FPF) (NYSE)

Chart Period: 10 years

Period High: $24.00 *Period Low:* $3.25

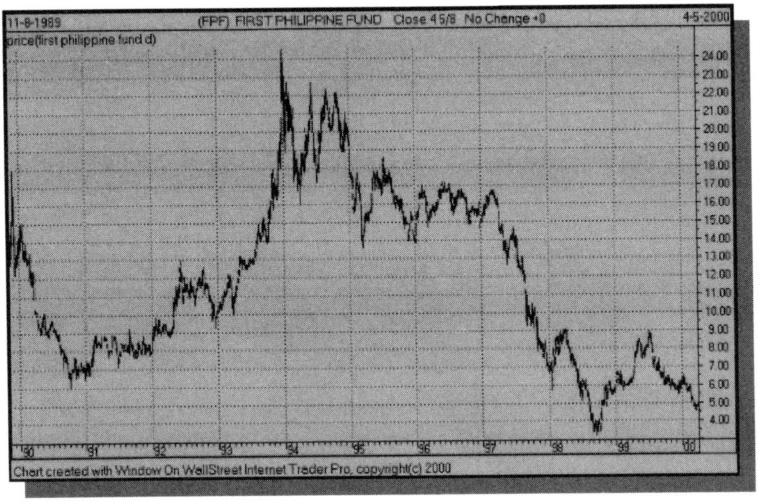

FIGURE 2.21 First Philippine Fund (FPF), 1990 to 2000.

Total Shares Outstanding: 11,225,000

Market Capitalization: $52,000,000

Fund Management: The First Philippine Fund, Inc. (400 Bellevue Parkway, 1st Floor, Wilmington, Delaware 19809, 800-810-9327)

SINGAPORE

FIGURE 2.22

Country Brief

Personal Thoughts: Like Hong Kong, Singapore is another strong Asian city-state. Actually, Singapore has a very mature, capitalistic economy, which is comparable to a Western developed economy. Not volatile, but a sure long-term bet.

Area: 647.5 square kilometers (slightly more than 3.5 times the size of Washington, D.C.)

Population: 3,490,356

Life Expectancy at Birth: 78.49 years

Ethnic Groups: Chinese 76.4%; Malay 14.9%; Indian 6.4%; other 2.3%

Religions: Buddhist (Chinese), Muslim (Malays), Christian, Hindu, Sikh, Taoist, Confucianist

Languages: Chinese (official), Malay (official and national), Tamil (official), English (official)

Literacy: 91.1%

Government Type: Republic within commonwealth

Economy Overview: Singapore has an open economy with strong service and manufacturing sectors and excellent international trading links derived from its entrepôt history. Extraordinarily strong fundamentals allowed Singapore to weather the effects of the Asian financial crisis better than its neighbors, but the crisis did pull GDP growth down to approximately 6 percent in 1997. Rising labor costs and appreciation of the Singapore dollar against its neighbors' currencies continue to be a threat to Singapore's competitiveness. The government's strategy to address this problem includes cutting costs, increasing productivity, improving infrastructure, and encouraging higher value-added industries. In applied technology, per-capita output, investment, and labor discipline, Singapore has key attributes of a developed country.

GDP/Real Growth Rate: $91.7 billion/1.3%

GDP—Per Capita: $24,600

GDP by Sector: Agriculture: negligible %; industry: 28%; services: 72%

Inflation Rate: –0.5%

Labor Force: 1.856 million

Unemployment Rate: 5%

Exports/Imports: $125.6 billion/$133.9 billion

Debt—External: NA

Military Expenditures/% of GDP: $4.03 billion/5.1%

Singapore's Index Funds: EWS and SGF

Singapore WEBS Index Series (EWS) (Nasdaq)

Chart Period: 4 years

Period High: $13.00 *Period Low:* $3.06

Total Shares Outstanding: 13,003,000

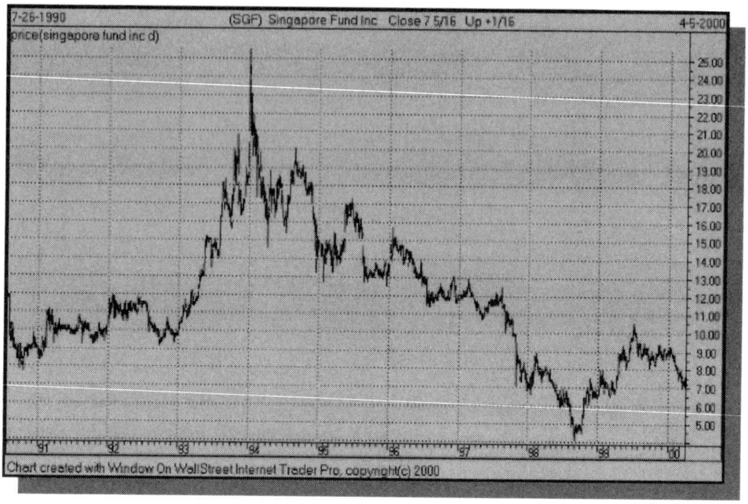

FIGURE 2.23 Singapore Fund, Inc. (SGF), 1990 to 2000.

Market Capitalization: \$92,000,000

Fund Management: WEBS Index Fund, Inc. (400 Bellevue Parkway, Wilmington, Delaware 19809, 800-810-9327)

The Singapore Fund, Inc. (SGF) (NYSE)

Chart Period: 11 years

Period High: \$25.50 *Period Low:* \$4.13

Total Shares Outstanding: 9,195,323

Market Capitalization: \$67,000,000

Fund Management: Daiwa Securities Trust Company (One Evertrust Plaza, Jersey City, New Jersey 07302)

TAIWAN

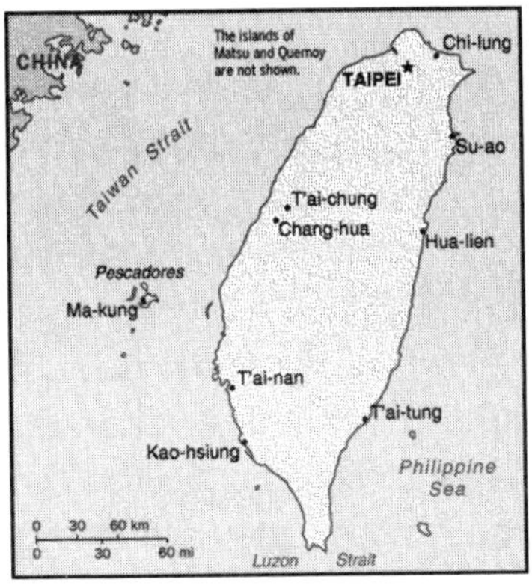

FIGURE 2.24

Country Brief

Personal Thoughts: Taiwan is similar in many ways to Hong Kong: very industrious people, and China wants to get its little commie hands on them! Excellent investment because of their short-term political instability (i.e., China) and long-term potential.

Area: 35,980 square kilometers (slightly smaller than Maryland and Delaware combined)

Population: 21,908,135

Life Expectancy at Birth: 76.82 years

Ethnic Groups: Taiwanese (including Hakka) 84%; mainland Chinese 14%; aborigine 2%

Religions: Mixture of Buddhist, Confucian, and Taoist 93%; Christian 4.5%; other 2.5%

Languages: Mandarin Chinese (official), Taiwanese (Min), Hakka dialects

Literacy: 86%

Government Type: Multiparty democratic regime headed by popularly elected president

Economy Overview: Taiwan has a dynamic capitalist economy with gradually decreasing guidance of investment and foreign trade by government authorities and partial government ownership of some large banks and industrial firms. Spillover from the Asian financial crisis hit Taiwan in the fourth quarter of 1997, wreaking havoc on the stock and currency markets. Increased export growth has provided the impetus for industrialization. Inflation and unemployment are low. Traditional labor-intensive industries are steadily being moved offshore and replaced with more capital- and technology-intensive industries. Taiwan has become a major investor in China, Thailand, Indonesia, the Philippines, Malaysia, and Vietnam. Because of its conservative financial approach and its entrepreneurial strengths, Taiwan suffered little compared with many of its neighbors from "the Asian flu" in 1998.

GDP/Real Growth Rate: $308 billion/4.8%

GDP—Per Capita: $16,200

GDP by Sector: Agriculture: 3.3%; industry: 35.7%; services: 61%

Inflation Rate: 0.9%

Labor Force: 9.4 million

Unemployment Rate: 2.7%

Exports/Imports: $122.1 billion/$114.4 billion

Debt—External: $80 million

Military Expenditures/% of GDP: $7.5 billion/2.6%

Taiwan's Index Funds: TWN and TYW

The Taiwan Fund, Inc. (TWN) (NYSE)

Chart Period: 13 years

Period High: $55.00 *Period Low:* $10.75

FIGURE 2.25 The Taiwan Fund, Inc. (TWN), 1987 to 2000.

Total Shares Outstanding: 16,365,572

Market Capitalization: $388,000,000

Fund Management: The Taiwan Fund, Inc. (225 Franklin Street, Boston, Massachusetts 02110, 800-426-5523)

The Singapore Fund, Inc. (TYW) (NYSE)

Chart Period: 5 years

Period High: $21.50 *Period Low:* $7.50

Total Shares Outstanding: 4,507,318

Market Capitalization: $89,6000,000

Fund Management: Daiwa Securities Trust Company (One Evertrust Plaza, Jersey City, New Jersey 07302)

THAILAND

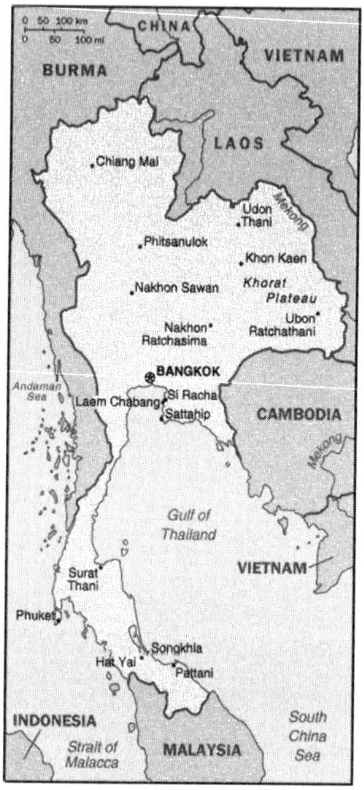

FIGURE 2.26

Country Brief

Personal Thoughts: Thailand is another personal favorite that has made lots of money for me in the past. Although I often question whether the government is in control of the growth, I have faith in the people and the culture.

Area: 514,000 square kilometers (slightly more than twice the size of Wyoming)

Population: 60,037,366

Life Expectancy at Birth: 69 years

Ethnic Groups: Thai 75%; Chinese 14%; other 11%

Religions: Mixture of Buddhist, Confucian, and Taoist 93%; Christian 4.5%; other 2.5%

Languages: Thai, English (secondary language of the elite), ethnic and regional dialects

Literacy: 93.8%

Government Type: Constitutional monarchy

Economy Overview: After months of speculative pressure on the Thai baht, the government decided to float the currency in July 1997, the symbolic beginning of the country's current economic crisis. The crisis—which began in the country's financial sector—spread throughout the economy. After years of rapid economic growth averaging 9 percent earlier in the 1990s, the Thai economy contracted 0.4 percent in 1997 and shrank another 8.5 percent in 1998. In the years before the crisis, Thailand ran persistent current account deficits. With the depreciation of the Thai baht and the collapse of domestic demand, however, imports fell off sharply—by more than 33 percent—and Thailand posted a trade surplus of approximately $12 billion in 1998. Foreign investment for new projects, the long-time catalyst of Thailand's economic growth, has also slowed. The government led by Prime Minister Chuan Lilephai has adhered closely to the economic recovery program prescribed by the International Monetary Fund. That cooperation afforded Thailand stability in the value of its currency in the second half of 1998 and helped replenish foreign reserves. Tough measures—including passage of adequate bankruptcy and foreclosure legislation as well as privatization of state-owned companies and recapitalization of the financial sector—remain to be accomplished. Bangkok also is trying to establish a social safety net for those displaced by the current economic crisis and is working to increase the quality of Thailand's labor force.

GDP/Real Growth Rate: $369 billion/–8.4%

GDP—Per Capita: $6,100

GDP by Sector: Agriculture: 10%; industry: 28.7%; services: 61.3%

Inflation Rate: 4.3%

Labor Force: 32.6 million

Unemployment Rate: 4.5%

Exports/Imports: $51.6 billion/$73.5 billion

Debt—External: $90 billion

Military Expenditures/% of GDP: $1.95 billion/2.5%

Thailand's Index Funds: TC & TTF

The Thai Capital Fund, Inc. (TC) (NYSE)

Chart Period: 12 years

Period High: $24.00 *Period Low:* $2.13

Total Shares Outstanding: 6,278,588

Market Capitalization: $22,400,000

Fund Management: Daiwa Securities Trust Company (One Evertrust Plaza, Jersey City, New Jersey 07302)

FIGURE 2.27 The Thai Fund, Inc. (TTF), 1988 to 2000.

The Thai Fund, Inc. (TTF) (NYSE)

Chart Period: 12 years

Period High: \$37.50 *Period Low:* \$3.75

Total Shares Outstanding: 13,267,712

Market Capitalization: \$77,300,000

Fund Management: Boston Equiserve (Investor Relations Department, P.O. Box 644, Boston, Massachusetts 02102-0644)

VIETNAM

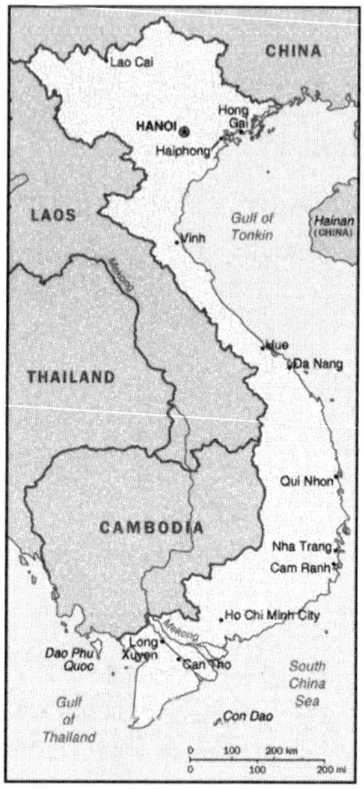

FIGURE 2.28

Country Brief

Personal Thoughts: Good luck, American cowboys! I wouldn't touch this with a 10-foot pole, except maybe for a quick buy and sell on an occasional drop.

Area: 329,560 square kilometers (slightly larger than New Mexico)

Population: 76,236,259

Life Expectancy at Birth: 67.74 years

Ethnic Groups: Vietnamese 85–90%; Chinese 3%; Muong, Tai, Meo, Khmer, Man, Cham (small percentages)

Religions: Buddhist, Taoist, Roman Catholic, indigenous beliefs, Islam, Protestant, Cao Dai, Hoa Hao

Languages: Vietnamese (official), Chinese, English, French, Khmer, tribal languages (Mon-Khmer and Malayo-Polynesian)

Literacy: 93.7%

Government Type: Communist state

Economy Overview: Vietnam is a poor, densely populated country that has had to recover from the ravages of war, the loss of financial support from the old Soviet bloc, and the rigidities of a centrally planned economy. Substantial progress has been achieved over the past 10 years in moving forward from an extremely low starting point. Economic growth continued at a strong pace during 1997 with industrial output rising by 12 percent and real GDP expanding by 8.5 percent. These positive numbers, however, masked some major difficulties that are emerging in economic performance. Many domestic industries, including coal, cement, steel, and paper, reported large stockpiles of inventory and tough competition from more efficient foreign producers, giving Vietnam a trade deficit of $3.3 billion in 1997. While disbursements of aid and foreign direct investment have risen, they are not large enough to finance the rapid increase in imports; and it is widely believed that Vietnam may be using short-term trade credits to bridge the gap—a risky strategy that could result in a foreign exchange crunch. Meanwhile, Vietnamese authorities continue to move slowly toward implementing the structural reforms needed to revitalize the economy and produce more competitive, export-driven industries. Privatization of state enterprises remains bogged down in political controversy, while the country's dynamic private sector is denied both financing and access to markets.

GDP/Real Growth Rate: $135 billion/4%

GDP—Per Capita: $1,700

GDP by Sector: Agriculture: 28%; industry: 30%; services: 42%

Inflation Rate: 9%

Labor Force: 32.7 million

Unemployment Rate: 25%

Exports/Imports: $7.1 billion/$11.1 billion

Debt: $7.3 billion Western countries; $4.5 billion Council for Mutual Economic Assistance (CEMA) debts primarily to Russia; $9 billion to $18 billion nonconvertible debt (former CEMA, Iraq, Iran)

Military Expenditures/% of GDP: $650 million/9.3%

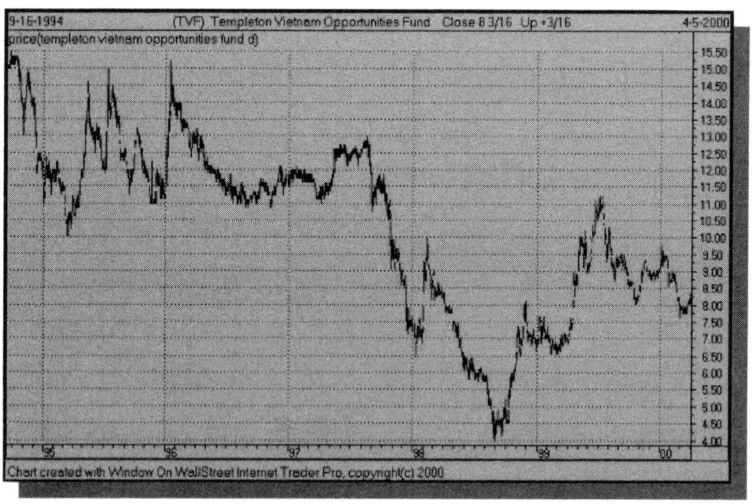

FIGURE 2.29 Templeton Vietnam and SE Asia Fund (TVF), 1995 to 2000.

Vietnam's Index Fund: TVF

Templeton Vietnam and SE Asia Fund (TVF) (NYSE)

Chart Period: 5 years

Period High: $15.50 *Period Low:* $4.00

Total Shares Outstanding: 4,681,173

Market Capitalization: $38,300,000

Fund Management: Templeton Vietnam Opportunity Fund, Inc. (700 Central Avenue, St. Petersburg, Florida 33701, 813-823-8712)

THE SOUTH AMERICAN MARKETS

FIGURE 2.30

ARGENTINA

FIGURE 2.31

Country Brief

Personal Thoughts: South America is the Asia of the Americas: developing and volatile. Although I am not as confident of South American economies as I am of those of Asia, South America still has a bright future. Argentina seems to be more of a stable bet than Brazil or Chile; it seems to have its political and economic situation more under control. Although I do not have any South American funds in my long-term portfolio right now (as the markets are a bit too high), I will be watching them closely for future buys.

Area: 2,766,890 square kilometers (slightly less than three-tenths the size of the United States)

Population: 36,265,463

Life Expectancy at Birth: 74.54 years

Ethnic Groups: White 85%; mestizo, Amerindian, or other non-white groups 15%

Religions: Nominally Roman Catholic 90% (less than 20% practicing); Protestant 2%; Jewish 2%; other 6%

Languages: Spanish (official), English, Italian, German, French

Literacy: 96.2%

Government Type: Republic

Economy Overview: Argentina benefits from rich natural resources, a highly literate population, an export-oriented agricultural sector, and a diversified industrial base. However, when President Carlos Menem took office in 1989, the country had piled up huge external debts, inflation had reached 200% per month, and output was plummeting. To combat the economic crisis, the government embarked on a path of trade liberalization, deregulation, and privatization. In 1991 it implemented radical monetary reforms that pegged the peso to the U.S. dollar and limited the growth in the monetary base by law to the growth in reserves. Inflation fell sharply in subsequent years. The Mexican peso crisis produced capital flight, the loss of banking system deposits, and a severe but short-lived recession in 1995; a series of reforms to bolster the domestic banking system followed. Real GDP growth recovered strongly, reaching almost 9 percent in 1997. In 1998 increasing investor anxiety over Brazil, its largest trading partner, produced the highest domestic interest rates in more than three years and slowed growth to 4.3 percent. Despite the relatively high level of growth in recent years, double-digit unemployment rates have persisted, largely because of rigidities in Argentina's labor laws.

GDP/Real Growth Rate: $348.2 billion/4.3%

GDP—Per Capita: $10,300

GDP by Sector: Agriculture: 7%; industry: 36%; services: 57%

Inflation Rate: 1%

Labor Force: 14.5 million

Unemployment Rate: 12%

Exports/Imports: $25.4 billion/$30.3 billion

Debt—External: $133 billion

Military Expenditures/% of GDP: $4.6 billion/1.5%

Argentina's Index Fund: AF

The Argentina Fund, Inc. (AF) (NYSE)

Chart Period: 8 years

Period High: $19.50 *Period Low:* $6.50

FIGURE 2.32 The Argentina Fund, Inc. (AF), 1992 to 2000.

Total Shares Outstanding: 9,273,027

Market Capitalization: $103,000,000

Fund Management: The Argentina Fund, Inc. (c/o Scudder Stevens & Clark, Ltd., 345 Park Avenue, New York, New York 10154, 212-326-6200)

BRAZIL

FIGURE 2.33

Country Brief

Personal Thoughts: Great for its tremendous volatility. But I have been caught numerous times holding on to the Brazil Fund much longer than I had planned. For some reason, Brazil does not follow the likely course predicted by my statistical indicators.

Area: 8,511,965 square kilometers (slightly smaller than the United States)

Population: 169,806,557

Life Expectancy at Birth: 64.36 years

Ethnic Groups: White (includes Portuguese, German, Italian, Spanish, Polish) 55%; mixed white and black 38%; black 6%; other (includes Japanese, Arab, Amerindian) 1%

Religions: Roman Catholic (nominal) 70%

Languages: Portuguese (official), English, Italian, German, French

Literacy: 83.3%

Government Type: Federal republic

Economy Overview: Possessing large and well-developed agricultural, mining, manufacturing, and service sectors, Brazil's economy outweighs that of all other South American countries and is expanding its presence in world markets. Prior to the institution of a stabilization plan—the Plano Real (Real Plan)—in mid-1994, stratospheric inflation rates had disrupted economic activity and discouraged foreign investment. Since then tight monetary policy has brought inflation under control: Consumer prices increased by 2 percent in 1998 compared to more than 1,000 percent in 1994. At the same time, GDP growth slowed from 5.7 percent in 1994 to about 3.0 percent in 1997 due to tighter credit. The Real Plan faced its strongest challenge in 1998, as the world financial crisis caused investors to examine the country's structural weaknesses more closely. The most severe spillover for Brazil—after Russia's debt default in August 1998—created unrelenting pressure on the currency, which forced the country to hike annual interest rates to 50 percent. Approximately $30 billion in capital left the country in August and September. After crafting a fiscal adjustment program and pledging progress on structural reform, Brazil received a $41.5 billion International Monetary Fund–led international support program in November 1998. Capital continued to leach out of the country, and investors, concerned about the rising mountain of debt and currency widely viewed as overvalued, stayed on the sidelines. In January 1999 Brazil made an abrupt shift of course in exchange rate policy, abandoning the strong currency anti-inflation anchor of the Real Plan. On January 13, 1999, Central Bank officials announced a one-time 8 percent devaluation of the real, and on January 15, 1999, the currency was declared to be freely floating. President Cardoso remains committed to limiting inflation and weathering the financial crisis through austerity and sacrifice as the country rides out a deep recession. He still hopes to address mandated revenue sharing with the states and cumbersome procedures to amend the constitution before the end of his second term.

GDP/Real Growth Rate: \$1.04 trillion/0.5%

GDP—Per Capita: \$6,300

GDP by Sector: Agriculture: 13%; industry: 38%; services: 49% (1995)

Inflation Rate: 2%

Labor Force: 57 million

Unemployment Rate: 2%

Exports/Imports: \$53 billion/\$61.4 billion

Debt—External: \$192.9 billion

Military Expenditures/% of GDP: \$15.1 billion/1.9%

FIGURE 2.34 The Brazil Fund, Inc. (BZF), 1991 to 2000.

Brazil's Index Funds: BZF and BZL

The Brazil Fund, Inc. (BZF) (NYSE)

Chart Period: 8 years

Period High: $36.00 *Period Low:* $6.50

Total Shares Outstanding: 16,300,000

Market Capitalization: $264,000,000

Fund Management: The Brazil Fund, Inc. (345 Park Avenue, New York, New York 10154, 800-349-4281)

Brazilian Equity Fund, Inc. (BZL) (Nasdaq)

Chart Period: 8 years

Period High: $27.00 *Period Low:* $3.00

Total Shares Outstanding: 4,607,000

Market Capitalization: $27,080,625

Fund Management: NA

CHILE

FIGURE 2.35

Country Brief

Personal Thoughts: I don't think I have ever invested in Chile. If you compare the Chile Fund's chart to the Argentina and Brazil funds, you will see that there is not as much volatility. And volatility is key for short- and medium-term profits (using my strategy, at least).

Area: 756,950 square kilometers (slightly smaller than twice the size of Montana)

Population: 14,787,781

Life Expectancy at Birth: 75.16 years

Ethnic Groups: White and white-Amerindian 95%; Amerindian 3%; other 2%

Religions: Roman Catholic 89%, Protestant 11%

Languages: Spanish

Literacy: 95.2%

Government Type: Republic

Economy Overview: Chile has a prosperous, essentially free market economy. Civilian governments—which took over from the military in March 1990—have continued to reduce the government's role in the economy while shifting the emphasis of public spending toward social programs. Growth in real GDP averaged more than 7.0 percent between 1991 and 1997 but fell to about half of that average in 1998 because of spillover from the global financial crisis. Inflation has been on a downward *trend* and hit a 60-year low in 1998. Chile's currency and foreign reserves also are strong, as sustained foreign capital inflows—including significant direct investment—have more than offset current account deficits and public debt buy-backs. President Frei, who took office in March 1994, has placed improving Chile's education system and developing foreign export markets at the top of his economic agenda. The Chilean economy remains largely dependent on a few sectors, particularly copper mining, fishing, and forestry. Success in meeting the government's goal of sustained annual economic growth of 5 percent depends largely on world prices for these commodities, continued foreign investor confidence, and the government's ability to maintain a conservative fiscal stance. In 1996 Chile became an associate member of Mercosur (Mercado Comun del Cono Sur—Southern Cone Common Market) and concluded a free trade agreement with Canada.

> **trend** the current general direction of movement for prices or rates.

GDP/Real Growth Rate: $184 billion/3.5%

GDP—Per Capita: $11,600

GDP by Sector: Agriculture: 8%; industry: 33%; services: 59%

Inflation Rate: 4.7%

Labor Force: 5.7 million

Unemployment Rate: 6.1%

Exports/Imports: $16.9 billion/$18.2 billion

Debt—External: $26.7 billion

Military Expenditures/% of GDP: $2.8 billion/3.5%

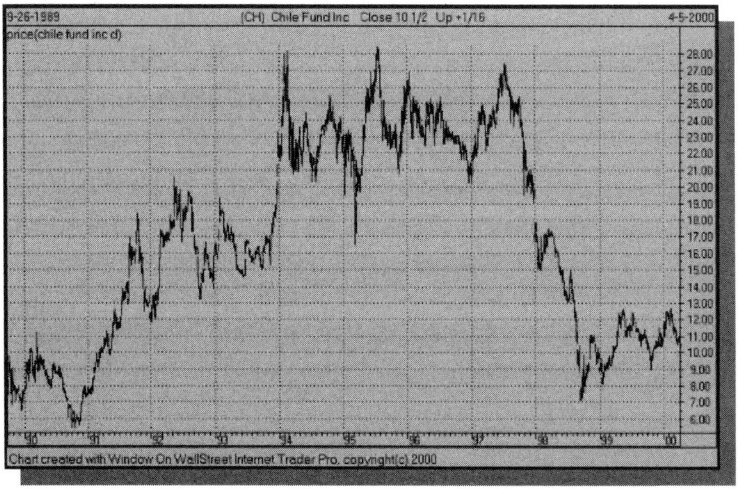

FIGURE 2.36 The Chile Fund, Inc. (CH), 1990 to 2000.

Chile's Index Fund: CH

The Chile Fund, Inc. (CH) (NYSE)

Chart Period: 11 years

Period High: $28.00 *Period Low:* $5.50

Total Shares Outstanding: 14,105,288

Market Capitalization: 149,000,000

Fund Management: Credit Suisse Asset Management (153 E. 53rd Street, New York, New York 10022)

MEXICO

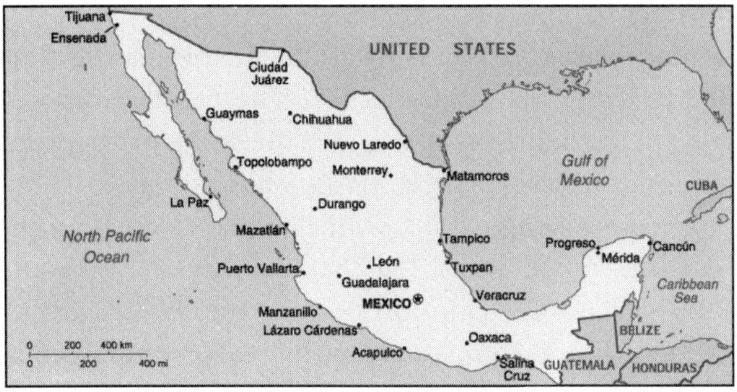

FIGURE 2.37

Country Brief

Personal Thoughts: Now, Mexico is a South American country I feel very confident in for short-, medium-, and long-term investments. Of course Mexico has its problems, but how could *any* country so close to America *not* do well?

Area: 1,972,550 square kilometers (slightly less than three times the size of Texas)

Population: 98,552,776

Life Expectancy at Birth: 71.63 years

Ethnic Groups: Mestizo (Amerindian-Spanish) 60%; Amerindian or predominantly Amerindian 30%; white 9%; other 1%

Religions: Nominally Roman Catholic 89%; Protestant 6%

Languages: Spanish, various Maya, Nahuatl, and other regional indigenous languages

Literacy: 89.6%

Government Type: Federal republic operating under a centralized government

Economy Overview: Mexico has a free market economy with a mixture of modern and outmoded industry and agriculture, increasingly dominated by the private sector. The number of state-owned enterprises in Mexico has fallen from more than 1,000 in 1982 to fewer than 200 in 1998. The Zedillo administration is privatizing and expanding competition in seaports, railroads, telecommunications, electricity, natural gas distribution, and airports. A strong export sector helped to cushion the economy's decline in 1995 and led the recovery in 1996 and 1997. In 1998 private consumption became the leading driver of growth, which was accompanied by increased employment and higher wages. The government expects the economy to slow in 1999 because of low commodity prices, tighter international liquidity, and slacker demand for exports. Mexico still needs to overcome many structural problems as it strives to modernize its economy and raise living standards. Income distribution is very unequal, with the top 20 percent of income earners accounting for 55 percent of income. Trade with the United States and Canada has nearly doubled since the North American Free Trade Agreement (NAFTA) was implemented in 1994. Mexico is pursuing additional trade agreements with most countries in Latin America and with the European Union to lessen its dependence on the United States.

GDP/Real Growth Rate: $815 billion/4.8%

GDP—Per Capita: $8,300

GDP by Sector: Agriculture: 8%; industry: 33%; services: 59%

Inflation Rate: 18.6%

Labor Force: 36.6 million

Unemployment Rate: 2.6%

Exports/Imports: $110.4 billion/$109.8 billion

Debt—External: $162 billion

Military Expenditures/% of GDP: $6 billion/1.3%

FIGURE 2.38 The Mexico Fund, Inc. (MXF), 1996 to 2000.

Mexico's Index Funds: EWW and MXF

Mexico WEBS Index Series (EWW) (Nasdaq)

Chart Period: 4 years

Period High: $20.75 *Period Low:* $7.00

Total Shares Outstanding: 13,003,000

Market Capitalization: $233,000,000

Fund Management: WEBS Index Fund, Inc. (400 Bellevue Parkway, Wilmington, Delaware 19809, 800-810-9327)

The Mexico Fund, Inc. (MXF) (NYSE)

Chart Period: 4 years

Period High: $23.00 *Period Low:* $7.56

Total Shares Outstanding: 50,763,316

Market Capitalization: $819,000,000

Fund Management: The Mexico Fund, Inc. (77 Aristotle's Street, 3rd Floor, Polanco, Mexico 11560)

AFRICA AND THE MIDDLE EAST MARKETS

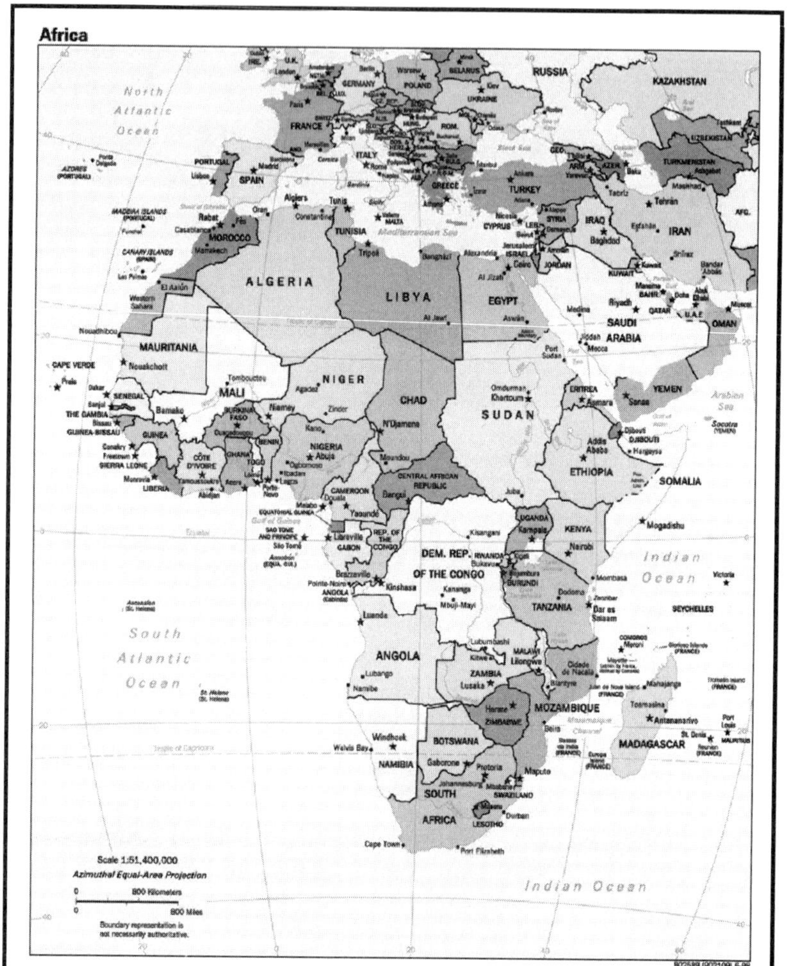

FIGURE 2.39

ISRAEL

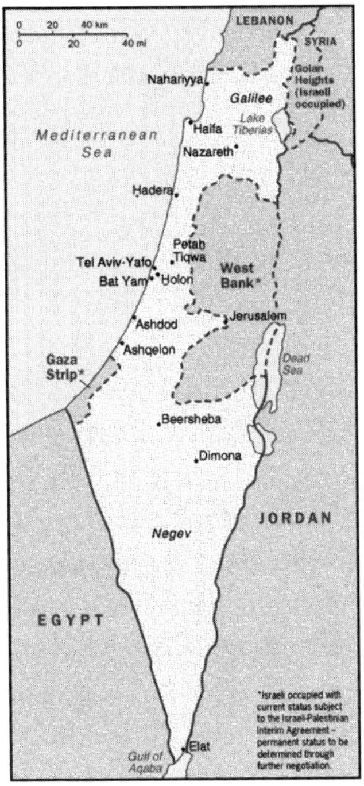

FIGURE 2.40

Country Brief

Personal Thoughts: I'm not putting my money in a country that spends nearly 10% of its GDP on military expenditures. Now, that's risky!

Area: 20,770 square kilometers (slightly smaller than New Jersey)

Population: 5,643,966

Life Expectancy at Birth: 78.41 years

Ethnic Groups: Jewish 82% (Israel-born 50%; Europe/Americas/Oceania-born 20%; Africa-born 7%; Asia-born 5%), non-Jewish 18% (mostly Arab)

Religions: Judaism 82%; Islam 14% (mostly Sunni Muslim); Christian 2%; Druze and other 2%

Languages: Hebrew (official); Arabic used officially for Arab minority; English most commonly used foreign language

Literacy: 95%

Government Type: Republic

Economy Overview: Israel has a technologically advanced market economy with substantial government participation. It depends on imports of crude oil, grains, raw materials, and military equipment. Despite limited natural resources, Israel has intensively developed its agricultural and industrial sectors over the past 20 years. Manufacturing and construction employ about 28 percent of Israeli workers; agriculture, forestry, and fishing only 2.6 percent; and services the rest. Diamonds, high-technology equipment, and agricultural products (fruits and vegetables) are leading exports. Israel usually posts sizable current account deficits, which are covered by large transfer payments from abroad and by foreign loans. Roughly half of the government's external debt is owed to the United States, which is its major source of economic and military aid.

GDP/Real Growth Rate: $96.7 billion/1.9%

GDP—Per Capita: $17,500

GDP by Sector: Agriculture: 2%; industry: 17%; services: 81%

Inflation Rate: 5.4%

Labor Force: 2.3 million

Unemployment Rate: 7.7%

Exports/Imports: $20.7 billion/$28.6 billion

Debt—External: $18.7 billion

Military Expenditures/% of GDP: $9.3 billion/9.5%

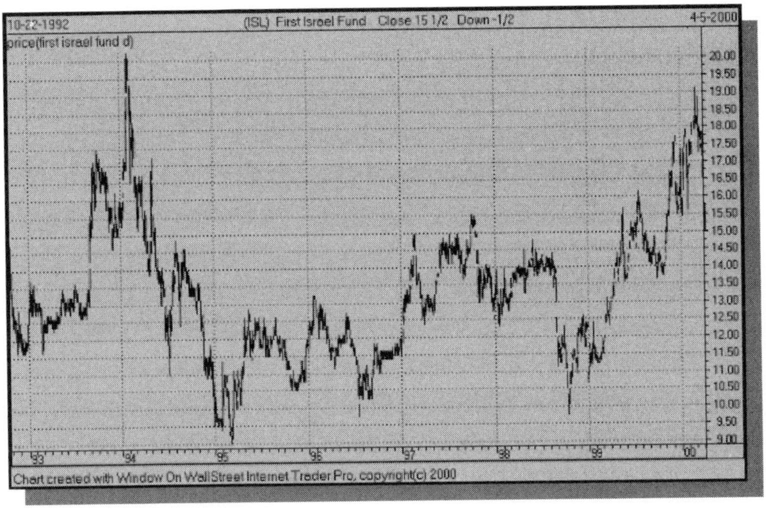

FIGURE 2.41 First Israel Fund (ISL), 1993 to 2000.

Israel's Index Fund: ISL

First Israel Fund (ISL) (NYSE)

Chart Period: 7 years

Period High: $21.00 *Period Low:* $9.00

Total Shares Outstanding: 4,890,194

Market Capitalization: $71,734,250

Fund Management: Credit Suisse Asset Management (153 E. 53rd Street, New York, New York 10022)

SOUTH AFRICA

FIGURE 2.42

Country Brief

Personal Thoughts: Slow growth. High inflation. Civil strife. I would rather put my money in Asia and South America.

Area: 1,219,912 square kilometers (slightly less than twice the size of Texas)

Population: 42,834,520

Life Expectancy at Birth: 55.65 years

Ethnic Groups: Black 75.2%; white 13.6%; non-white 8.6%; Indian 2.6%

Religions: Christian 68% (includes most whites and coloreds, about 60% of blacks and about 40% of Indians); Muslim 2%; Hindu 1.5% (60% of Indians); traditional and animistic 28.5%

Languages: 11 official languages, including Afrikaans, English, Ndebele, Pedi, Sotho, Swazi, Tsonga, Tswana, Venda, Xhosa, Zulu

Literacy: 81.8%

Government Type: Republic

Economy Overview: South Africa is a middle-income, developing country with an abundant supply of resources; well-developed financial, legal, communications, energy, and transport sectors; a stock exchange that ranks among the 10 largest in the world; and a modern infrastructure supporting an efficient distribution of goods to major urban centers throughout the region. Growth has been positive since the historic election of President Nelson Mandela in the country's first multiracial elections in 1994 but not strong enough to cut into the substantial unemployment. Daunting economic problems remain from the apartheid era, especially the problems of poverty and economic empowerment among the blacks. Other problems are crime and corruption. The new South African government demonstrated its commitment to open markets, privatization, and a favorable investment climate with the release of its macroeconomic strategy in June 1996.

GDP/Real Growth Rate: $270 billion/0.3%

GDP—Per Capita: $6,200

GDP by Sector: Agriculture: 5%; industry: 37%; services: 58%

Inflation Rate: 9.7%

Labor Force: 14.2 million

Unemployment Rate: 30%

Exports/Imports: $31.3 billion/$28 billion

Debt—External: $23.5 billion

Military Expenditures/% of GDP: $2 billion/2.2%

Africa's Index Funds: AFF and SOA

Morgan Stanley Dean Witter Africa Investment Fund, Inc. (AFF) (NYSE)

Chart Period: 6 years

Period High: $18.00 *Period Low:* $8.06

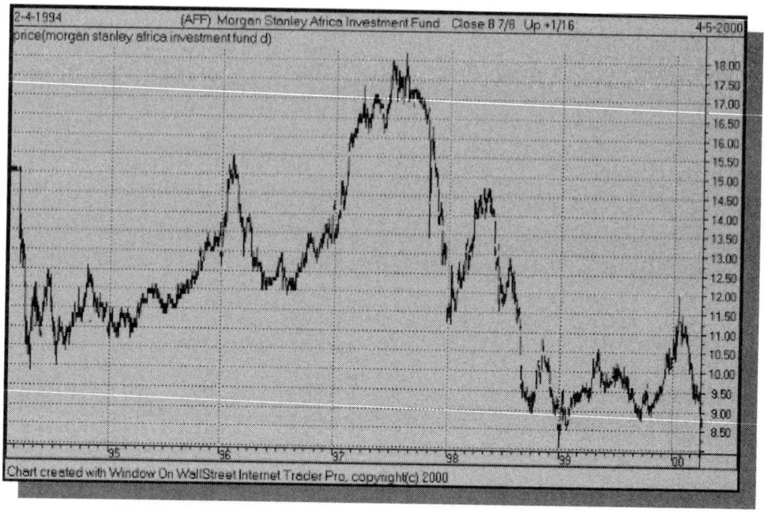

FIGURE 2.43 Morgan Stanley Africa Investment Fund, Inc. (AFF), 1994 to 2000.

Total Shares Outstanding: 14,041,122

Market Capitalization: 137,000,000

Fund Management: American Stock Transfer and Trust Company (40 Wall Street, New York, New York 10005)

The Southern Africa Fund, Inc. (SOA) (NYSE)

Chart Period: 6 years

Period High: $20.00 *Period Low:* $7.13

Total Shares Outstanding: 6,007,100

Market Capitalization: $87,900,000

Fund Management: Alliance Capital Management (1345 Avenue of the Americas, 31st Floor, New York, New York 10105)

"DEVELOPING" EUROPEAN MARKETS

FIGURE 2.44

PORTUGAL

FIGURE 2.45

Country Brief

Personal Thoughts: Okay, so Portugal and Spain are not really "emerging" markets. But they are just so far behind other developed countries, I had to include them. I don't think I have ever invested in them.

Area: 92,391 square kilometers (slightly smaller than Indiana)

Population: 9,927,556

Life Expectancy at Birth: 75.66 years

Ethnic Groups: Homogeneous Mediterranean stock in mainland, Azores, Madeira Islands; citizens of black African descent who immigrated to mainland during decolonization number fewer than 100,000

Religions: Roman Catholic 97%; Protestant denominations 1%; other 2%

Languages: Portuguese

Literacy: 85%

Government Type: Parliamentary democracy

Economy Overview: Portugal, in 1998, continued to see strong economic growth, falling interest rates, and low unemployment. The country qualified for the European Monetary Union (EMU) in 1998 and joined with 10 other European countries in launching the euro on January 1, 1999. Portugal's inflation rate for 1998, 2.8 percent, was low but higher than most of its European partners. The country continues to run a trade deficit and a balance-of-payments deficit. The government is working to modernize capital plant and increase the country's competitiveness in the increasingly integrated world markets. Growth is expected to slow to 3 percent in 1999 because of a slowdown in public investment and sluggish demand for exports.

GDP/Real Growth Rate: $149.5 billion/4.2%

GDP—Per Capita: $14,600

GDP by Sector: Agriculture: 6%; industry: 36%; services: 58% (1995 est.)

Inflation Rate: 2.3%

Labor Force: 4.53 million

Unemployment Rate: 5%

Exports/Imports: $23.8 billion/$33.9 billion

Debt—External: $13.1 billion

Military Expenditures/% of GDP: $2.5 billion/2.6%

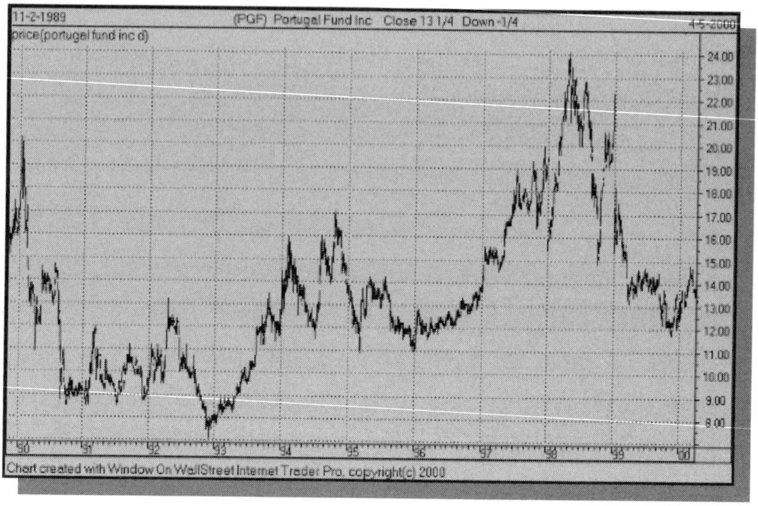

FIGURE 2.46 The Portugal Fund, Inc. (PGF), 1990 to 2000.

Portugal's Index Fund: PGF

The Portugal Fund, Inc. (PGF) (NYSE)

Chart Period: 10 years

Period High: $24.00 *Period Low:* $7.25

Total Shares Outstanding: 5,328,316

Market Capitalization: $70,800,000

Fund Management: Credit Suisse Asset Management (153 E. 53rd Street, New York, New York 10022)

RUSSIA

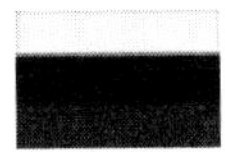

FIGURE 2.47

Country Brief

Personal Thoughts: If you ever wished that you were one of Al Capone's cronies, here is your chance: Russia is a country run by the KGB-turned-mobsters. Russia is good for short-term plays, but I am not sure I would invest in it for too long.

Area: 17,075,200 square kilometers (slightly less than 1.8 times the size of the United States)

Population: 146,861,022

Life Expectancy at Birth: 64.97 years

Ethnic Groups: Russian 81.5%; Tatar 3.8%; Ukrainian 3%; Chuvash 1.2%; Bashkir 0.9%; Byelorussian 0.8%; Moldavian 0.7%; other 8.1%

Religions: Russian Orthodox, Muslim, other

Languages: Russian, other

Literacy: 98%

Government Type: Federation

Economy Overview: Seven years after the collapse of the Soviet Union, Russia is still struggling to establish a modern market economy and achieve strong economic growth. Russian GDP has contracted an estimated 43 percent since 1991, including a 5 percent drop in 1998, despite the country's wealth of natural resources, its well-educated population, and its diverse—although increasingly dilapidated—industrial base. By the end of 1997, Russia had achieved some progress. Inflation had been brought under control, the ruble was stabilized, and an ambitious privatization program had transferred thousands of enterprises to private ownership. Some important market-oriented laws also were passed, including a commercial code governing business relations and an arbitration court for resolving economic disputes. But in 1998 the Asian financial crisis swept through the country, contributing to a sharp decline in Russia's earnings from oil exports and resulting in an exodus of foreign investors. Matters came to a head in August 1998, when the government allowed the ruble to fall precipitously and stopped payment on $40 billion in ruble bonds. Ongoing problems include an undeveloped legal and financial system, poor progress on restructuring the military-industrial complex, and persistently large budget deficits, largely reflecting the inability of successive governments to collect sufficient taxes. Russia's transition to a market economy also has been slowed by the growing prevalence of payment arrears and barter and by widespread corruption. The severity of Russia's economic problems is dramatized by the large annual decline in population, estimated by some observers at 800,000 people, caused by environmental hazards, the decline in healthcare, and the unwillingness of people to have children.

GDP/Real Growth Rate: $692 billion/–5%

GDP—Per Capita: $4,000

GDP by Sector: Agriculture: 7%; industry: 39%; services: 54%

Inflation Rate: 84%

Labor Force: 66 million

Unemployment Rate: 11.5%

Exports/Imports: $86.7 billion/$66.9 billion

Military Expenditures: NA

Russia's Index Funds: RNE and TRF

Morgan Stanley Russia and New Europe Fund, Inc. (RNE) (NYSE)

Chart Period: 3 years

Period High: $42.00 *Period Low:* $6.88

Total Shares Outstanding: 5,037,748

Market Capitalization: $90,100,000

Fund Management: American Stock Transfer and Trust Company (40 Wall Street, New York, New York 10005)

FIGURE 2.48 Morgan Stanley Russia and New Europe Fund (RNE), 1997 to 2000.

Templeton Russia Fund, Inc. (TRF) (NYSE)

Chart Period: 4 years

Period High: $65.00 *Period Low:* $6.06

Total Shares Outstanding: 5,415,714

Market Capitalization: $89,900,000

Fund Management: Templeton Russia Fund, Inc. (700 Central Avenue, St. Petersburg, Florida 33701, 813-823-8712)

SPAIN

FIGURE 2.49

Country Brief

Personal Thoughts: See Portugal.

Area: 504,750 square kilometers (slightly more than twice the size of Oregon)

Population: 39,133,996

Life Expectancy at Birth: 77.56 years

Ethnic Groups: Composite of Mediterranean and Nordic types

Religions: Roman Catholic 99%; other 1%

Languages: Castilian Spanish 74%; Catalan 17%; Galician 7%; Basque 2%

Literacy: 96%

Government Type: Parliamentary monarchy

Economy Overview: Spain's mixed capitalist economy supports a GDP that on a per-capita basis is three-fourths that of the four leading West European economies. Its center-right government has staked much on gaining admission to the first group of countries to implement the European single currency, and, based on economic indicators, Madrid appears poised to be in the European Monetary Union from the outset. Unemployment, nonetheless, remains the highest in the European Union, at 21 percent. The government, for political reasons, has made only limited progress in changing labor laws and reforming pension schemes, which are key to the sustainability of both Spain's internal economic advances and its competitiveness in a single currency area.

GDP/Real Growth Rate: $642.4 billion/3.3%

GDP—Per Capita: $16,400

GDP by Sector: Agriculture: 3.6%; industry: 33.6%; services: 62.8%

Inflation Rate: 2.1%

Labor Force: 16.2 million

Unemployment Rate: 21%

Exports/Imports: $94.5 billion/$118.3 billion

Debt—External: $90 billion

Military Expenditures/% of GDP: $6.3 billion/1.4%

Spain's Index Funds: EWP and SNF

Spain WEBS Index Series (EWP) (Nasdaq)

Chart Period: 4 years

Period High: $33.00 *Period Low:* $13.40

Total Shares Outstanding: 13,003,000

Market Capitalization: $334,014,563

Fund Management: WEBS Index Fund, Inc. (400 Bellevue Parkway, Wilmington, Delaware 19809, 800-810-9327)

FIGURE 2.50 The Spain Fund, Inc. (SNF), 1989 to 2000.

The Spain Fund, Inc. (SNF) (NYSE)

Chart Period: 12 Years

Period High: $39.00 *Period Low:* $7.50

Total Shares Outstanding: 10,000,000

Market Capitalization: $137,000,000

Fund Management: Alliance Capital Management (1345 Avenue of the Americas, 31st Floor, New York, New York 10105)

TURKEY

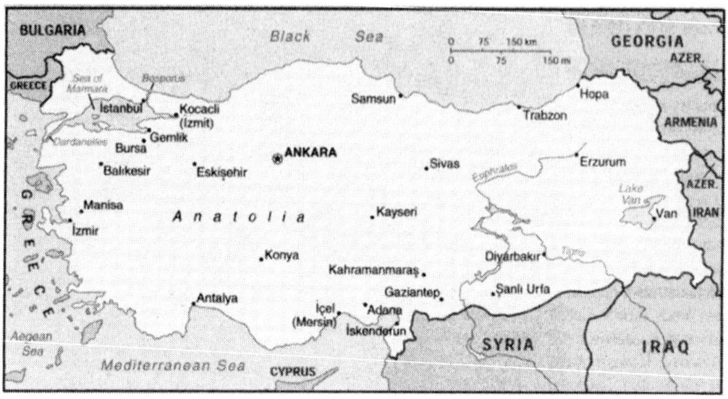

FIGURE 2.51

Country Brief

Personal Thoughts: As you can see from the chart for the Turkish Investment Fund, Turkey has not really done much in the last 10 years or so (except for a brief, albeit major, rise in late 1993). I am not sure if it will be a part of my long-term portfolio.

Area: 780,580 square kilometers (slightly larger than Texas)

Population: 64,566,511

Life Expectancy at Birth: 72.82 years

Ethnic Groups: Turkish 80%; Kurdish 20%

Religions: Muslim 99.8% (mostly Sunni); other 0.2% (Christian and Jews)

Languages: Turkish (official), Kurdish, Arabic

Literacy: 82.3%

Government Type: Republican parliamentary democracy

Economy Overview: Turkey's dynamic economy is a complex mix of modern industry and commerce along with traditional village agriculture and crafts. Turkey has a strong and rapidly growing private sector, yet the state still plays a major role in basic industry, banking, transport, and communication. Its most important industry—and the largest source of exports—is textiles and clothing, which is almost entirely in private hands. In recent years the economic situation has been marked by rapid growth coupled with partial success in implementing structural reform measures. Inflation declined to 70 percent in 1998, down from 99 percent in 1997, but the public sector fiscal deficit probably remained near 10 percent of GDP, due in large part to interest payments, which accounted for 42 percent of central government spending in 1998. The government enacted a new tax law and speeded up privatization in 1998 but made no progress on badly needed social security reform. Although Ankara is trying to increase trade with other countries in the region, most of Turkey's trade is still with member countries of the Organization for Economic Cooperation and Development. Despite the implementation in January 1996 of a customs union with the European Union, foreign direct investment in the country remains low—about $1 billion annually—perhaps because potential investors are concerned about still-high inflation and the unsettled political situation. Economic growth will remain about the same in 1999; inflation should decline further.

GDP/Real Growth Rate: $388.3 billion/7.2%

GDP—Per Capita: $6,100

GDP by Sector: Agriculture: 15%; industry: 28.4%; services: 56.6%

Inflation Rate: 99%

Labor Force: 21.6 million

Unemployment Rate: 5.9%

Exports/Imports: $26 billion/$46.7 billion

Debt—External: $84.5 billion

Military Expenditures/% of GDP: $4.3 billion/3.5%

FIGURE 2.52 The Turkish Investment Fund, Inc. (TKF), 1990 to 2000.

Turkey's Index Fund: TKF

The Turkish Investment Fund, Inc. (TKF) (NYSE)

Chart Period: 10 years

Period High: \$22.00 *Period Low:* \$3.81

Total Shares Outstanding: 6,586,880

Market Capitalization: \$116,000,000

Fund Management: Investors Bank and Trust Company (200 Clarendon Street, Boston, Massachusetts 02116)

Chapter 3

A New Toy: Investment Software

TIME TO GET BUSY

A few years ago I was reading a book written by two senior writers/editors of *The Wall Street Journal* entitled *The Book of International Investing: Everything You Need to Know About Investing in Foreign Markets*. At the time I was living in the United States producing television shows and wanted to get more involved with international investing again. I was so impressed with the book that I called the book's authors suggesting we create a television program around international investing.

I flew up to New York City from Washington, D.C., to meet John Prestbo and Doug Sease at their office. After our meeting, they handed me a copy of their most recent book, *Barron's Guide to Making Investment Decisions*. I highly recommend both of these books; they go into more detail about the variety of investment options than I can here.

Prestbo's and Sease's international book introduced me to the closed-end country funds. Although I conducted further research to get a list of the specific country funds and their stock *symbols*, I could not find this information anywhere. The many available books on electronic *day trades* and online *investing* did not go into the detail novices require to start investing from the ground up. Most investment books do not recommend investment software, or tell you how to use the software; and they do not explain, in simple language, the basics of purchasing, monitoring, and selling stocks online.

symbol a system of letters used to identify uniquely a stock or mutual fund.

day trade the purchase and sale of the same security on the same day.

investing using money to make more money, usually with the understanding that risk is something to be avoided unless adequately compensated for. Often done by purchasing items of value for income or capital appreciation, such as stocks, bonds, mutual funds, unit investment trusts, real estate, money market funds, and collectibles.

So I had to learn all of this on my own.

SOFTWARE

After creating a list of the single-country closed-end funds, the next step was to analyze each fund's data. I needed software for this. Only one company was distributing investment software for the nonprofessional investor—at least in retail stores. To this day, I have never seen other stock analysis software for sale in any computer store.

The software company is Window on Wall Street. The first package I purchased was a basic program. A few months later the company came out with an array of professional versions, starting at around $300, offered over their Internet site (www.windowonwallstreet.com). These new versions had significantly more analytic tools and the ability to get live data over the Internet. What this means is that users can get tick-by-tick, live, real-time stock quotes, like any professional broker on Wall Street. A good deal indeed!

The version I am using is Window on Wall Street Internet Trader Pro 7.0. Up until the end of 1999, you could purchase a very similar program for around $30 at your local discount computer store. Unfortunately, the industry has changed a lot since then and low-cost consumer versions are no longer available in retail stores. The industry has moved to web-based models, combining software and data together. I will discuss stock analysis options a little later in the chapter.

Once I had a list of single-country funds, I wanted to look at each country's stock market over a 10- to 20-year period. I had a feeling that, over time, international markets would move in predictable waves and that, if I applied the proper analytical tools, I could predict the ups and downs of these waves.

At the time—in 1997—long-term data were very hard to come by. Although many financial sites, such as Yahoo! and BigCharts.com, now offer long-term charts of these markets, then the data were available only from expensive financial research consultants and companies such as Reuters. Even large university libraries had no information available.

The Window on Wall Street software I originally purchased came with a CD with *historical data* for most American stocks listed on New York Stock Exchange, the American Stock Exchange, and Nasdaq. The data consisted of prices, *volume*, *earnings per share*, *dividends*, and more. This was all I needed for my analysis. Yahoo! had historical country index charts going back five years. I compared the country fund charts I created with my Window on Wall Street software with the country index charts from Yahoo!, and found that most country funds followed their respective indexes very closely. I did not need the hard-to-come-by 20-year country index data; the historical data from the index funds would work just fine.

historical data past information about a company, used to help forecast the company's future; for example, historical price, price/earnings ratio, revenues and revenue growth, earnings and earnings growth.

volume the number of shares, bonds, or contracts traded during a given period, for a security or an entire exchange.

earnings per share (EPS) total earnings divided by the number of shares outstanding. Companies often use a weighted average of outstanding stock over the reporting term.

dividend a taxable payment declared by a company's board of directors and given to its shareholders out of the company's current or retained earnings, usually quarterly. Usually it is given as cash (cash dividend), but it also can take the form of stock (stock dividend) or other property. Also called payout.

For example, compare Figures 3.1 and 3.2. I created Figure 3.1 using the Window on Wall Street program. It is a one-year chart of Templeton China World Fund (TCH). As I mentioned in Chapter 2,

FIGURE 3.1 Templeton China World, September 1998 to September 1999.

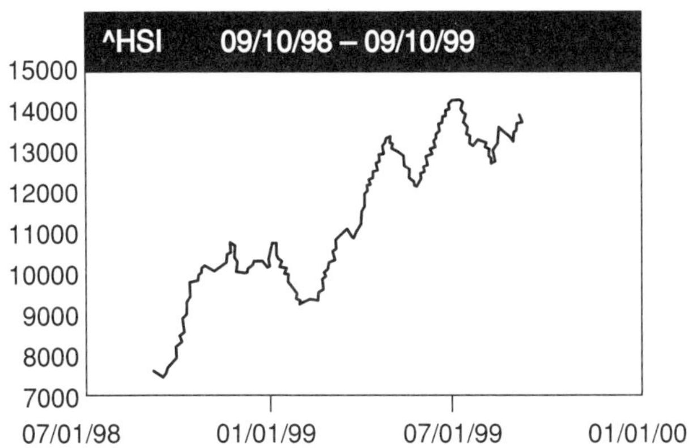

FIGURE 3.2 Hong Kong Hang Sang Index, September 1998 to September 1999.

many of the "China" funds consist mainly of stocks traded on Hong Kong's stock exchange. The second chart, obtained from MSNBC's web site, is the Hong Kong Hang Sang Index. While they are not identical, they are close. This was the case with the other country funds as well. Now that I had the historical data, I needed daily updates so I could follow the funds and apply analytical tools to real-life situations. Various online companies offered end-of-day downloads for $20 and up; today the situation has changed a bit. The product (software) and service (daily data) have merged. Now various companies (like Window on Wall Street) and online brokers offer the product and service together.

We will examine various service and product types so you can see the differences between basic tools and those that professional investors may use. The free services offered by many online sites may be all you need to create and manage a successful portfolio.

Please keep in mind the three major purposes of investment software: (1) to collect stock data, (2) to analyze the data, and (3) to monitor and manage a portfolio. The price of the products/services varies by degree of these three elements desired.

Data collection comes in four basic forms:

1. *Historical:* stock information from the past, often 20 years back
2. *Real time:* intraday data received immediately as it develops on Wall Street
3. *Delayed:* intraday data that are slightly aged, by 15 minutes or so
4. *End of day:* data received at the end of a business day (a little after 4:20—Nasdaq prices are not available as early as stocks traded on the NYSE)

delayed not current, as with quotes or news.

Although many companies offer investment software, service and product types fall into two basic categories: (1) tools for nonprofessional investors and (2) tools for professional investors. The main difference between the two is that tools designed for professional investors include the ability to receive and analyze "Level 2" data (detailed information on the movement of a stock, including buyers' and sellers' names/IDs, transaction amounts and sizes, and times of transactions) and include a greater variety of analytical tools.

NONPROFESSIONAL TOOLS

Stock analysis software and services offer a number of different functions, some of which nonprofessional users may not require.

These functions include:

- ✔ Streaming data
- ✔ Powerful charting
- ✔ Technical analysis
- ✔ Portfolio manager.

Streaming Data

If you plan on monitoring stock prices regularly throughout the day, as day traders do, or if you enjoy watching stock movements live, you certainly will want to purchase live "streaming" data. With streaming data, you can watch specific stocks as their prices and other data change in real time. Figure 3.3 shows a sample window from my Window on Wall Street program.

The person who set up this quote list has separated the stocks she is monitoring into three categories: (1) Technology Stocks, (2) Internet Stocks, and (3) Telecommunications. I maintain two quote lists—one with all of the international funds that I monitor regularly and the other with the stocks currently in my portfolio. The latter list is on my screen at all times. If I have money to spend and I am on the hunt, I look through the full list. If I am looking to buy one or more stocks in particular, I add a "Watch" category on my main window, under the "Own" category.

With the press of a button, you can easily perform market rankings to view the most active or biggest gainers on the NYSE, American

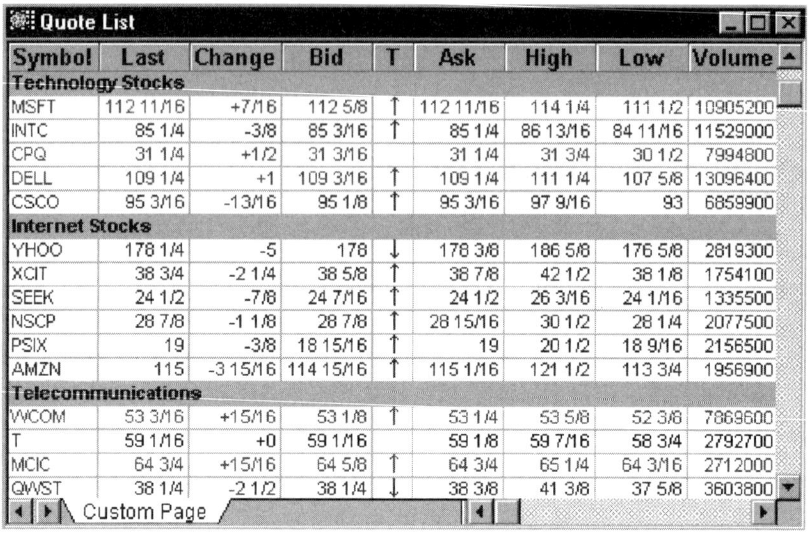

Quote List

Symbol	Last	Change	Bid	T	Ask	High	Low	Volume
Technology Stocks								
MSFT	112 11/16	+7/16	112 5/8	↑	112 11/16	114 1/4	111 1/2	10905200
INTC	85 1/4	-3/8	85 3/16	↑	85 1/4	86 13/16	84 11/16	11529000
CPQ	31 1/4	+1/2	31 3/16		31 1/4	31 3/4	30 1/2	7994800
DELL	109 1/4	+1	109 3/16	↑	109 1/4	111 1/4	107 5/8	13096400
CSCO	95 3/16	-13/16	95 1/8	↑	95 3/16	97 9/16	93	6859900
Internet Stocks								
YHOO	178 1/4	-5	178	↓	178 3/8	186 5/8	176 5/8	2819300
XCIT	38 3/4	-2 1/4	38 5/8	↑	38 7/8	42 1/2	38 1/8	1754100
SEEK	24 1/2	-7/8	24 7/16	↑	24 1/2	26 3/16	24 1/16	1335500
NSCP	28 7/8	-1 1/8	28 7/8	↑	28 15/16	30 1/2	28 1/4	2077500
PSIX	19	-3/8	18 15/16	↑	19	20 1/2	18 9/16	2156500
AMZN	115	-3 15/16	114 15/16	↑	115 1/16	121 1/2	113 3/4	1956900
Telecommunications								
WCOM	53 3/16	+15/16	53 1/8	↑	53 1/4	53 5/8	52 3/8	7869600
T	59 1/16	+0	59 1/16		59 1/8	59 7/16	58 3/4	2792700
MCIC	64 3/4	+15/16	64 5/8	↑	64 3/4	65 1/4	64 3/16	2712000
QWST	38 1/4	-2 1/2	38 1/4	↓	38 3/8	41 3/8	37 5/8	3603800

Custom Page

FIGURE 3.3 Quote list.

Stock Exchange (AMEX), or Nasdaq—the program is fully customizable and updates automatically. Much like a spreadsheet, the quote list uses columns to display over 45 data points, such as bid (sell price), ask (buy price), EPS (earnings per share), percent change, volume, and much more. To add a security, you simply type in the symbol, and the information will be retrieved and automatically updated.

Window on Wall Street now offers software for free, with a monthly subscription charge of $70 for streaming data. The company's main competitor is eSignal by MetaStock (www.esignal.com). That software costs around $400, with a monthly subscription of $300 or so. Dozens of other companies offer stock analysis software, but they have big price tags, and you have to purchase the data separately from another source. (FYI: Many software companies advertise in *Stocks and Commodities* magazine.)

Does that mean that I recommend Window on Wall Street? Although I do like the product, there are other free options you should consider. On-line brokers now are offering free streaming data services to their customers. In Chapter 6 I review a number of online brokers and mention which ones offer this service.

Another powerful feature of many of these programs is that you can set an alarm to go off if a stock hits a certain point. This is crucial if you do not want to waste your time sitting at the computer watching data move up and down all day. When I am looking to buy or sell a security, I often set an alarm to go off when it reaches a certain price. Then I can conduct research to get a better feel of the market—to see which way I think the market is moving, and to decide if I should wait or make my move now. (Somtimes I decide ahead of time to buy or sell at a particular price regardless of how the market moves. In that case I set a "limit" order, which we will discuss in more detail in Chapter 5.) Most free services do *not* offer the alarm feature.

Powerful Charting

Charting is a major feature of investment software. Good charting capabilities are essential for market analysis. A *chart* usually is founded on a stock's price and volume. From there, you can add windows for various analytical tools, which we will discuss soon. Figure 3.4 presents a basic window, a chart of Disney. The upper portion of the chart shows the stock's price movements over time. The lower portion charts its volume over time. (Volume is the number of shares traded on each day. The higher the line, the more stocks that were traded on a particular day.)

chart a graph of the price movements of a given security over a given time period, sometimes along with volume data.

Investment software varies in the amount of analytical tools available. Figure 3.5 shows an analytical tool added to a chart. The solid line is an average of prices over a period of time, so you can see how a

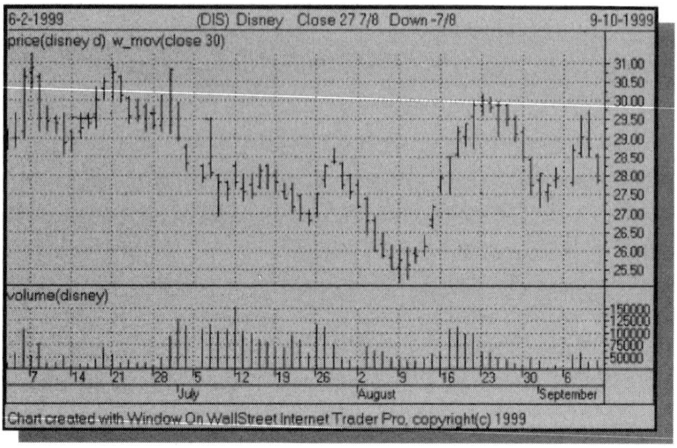

FIGURE 3.4 Disney chart 1.

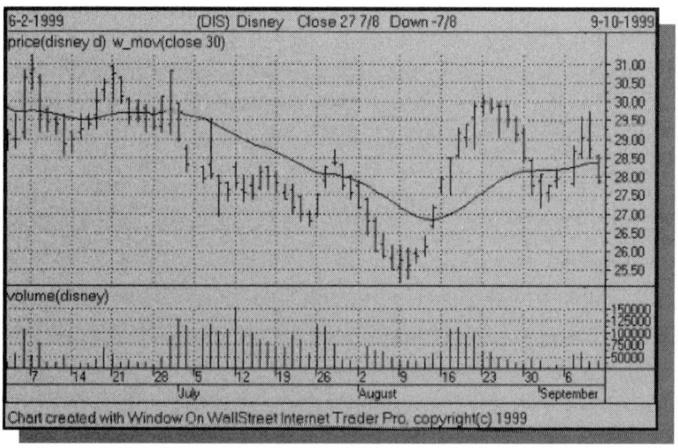

FIGURE 3.5 Disney chart 2.

stock's price at a particular time compares with the average price over a period of time.

You also can add a new window for an analytical tool. Figure 3.6 shows the "money flow index," which we will discuss in Chapter 4.

Another nice chart you can create with your software is an intraday chart, shown in Figure 3.7. You usually have to pay a little more for

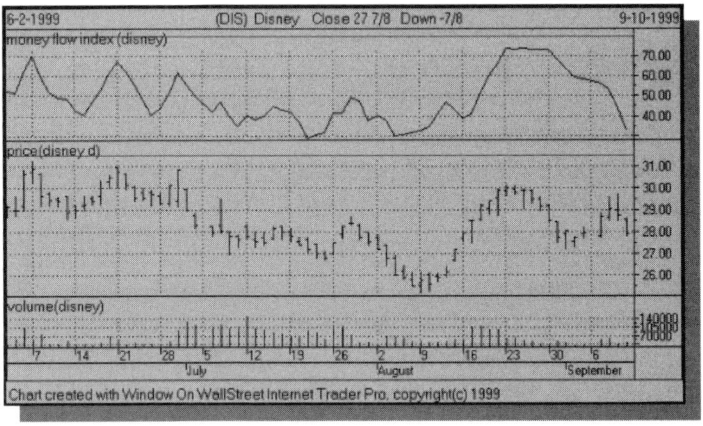

FIGURE 3.6 Intraday chart.

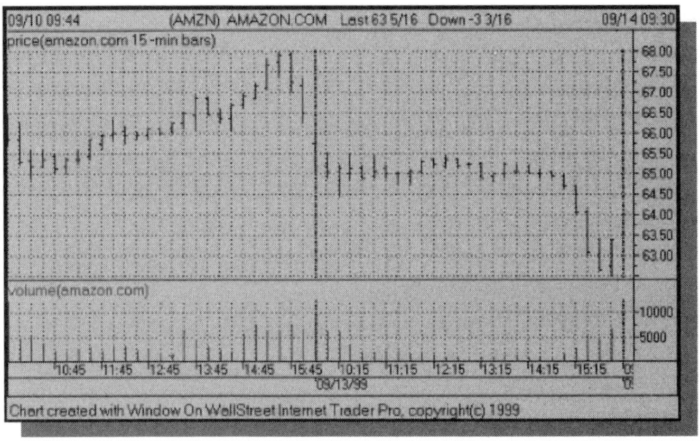

FIGURE 3.7 Amazon.com price and volume chart.

this option. The figure shows a two-day price and volume chart of Amazon.com. As stock prices usually move in waves, not mere random jumps, often it is useful to see how a stock's price is moving over a shorter time frame than other types (weekly, yearly, monthly, etc.). This may be beneficial during very active periods when one wishes to buy or sell a security.

My computer is set so that at the end of each market day, it automatically downloads data for the 100 or so stocks I monitor on a daily basis. Then, sometime in the evening, I spend about 10 to 15 minutes looking through the charts.

Stock charts are available free of charge on many web sites, from search engines like Yahoo! and AOL, to financial sites like CNNfn and *The Wall Street Journal*. All online brokers offer this service. However, most of these sites have limited analytical tools and capabilities.

One of the most powerful sites is BigCharts.com. This is a free site, with more analytical tools than you will need for country funds. Big Charts' users can select from a long list of analytical tools, time periods, and even chart background colors and images. For free!

The only major drawback to using a free service is that it takes a great deal of time to review end-of-day charts. At BigCharts, for example, users must type in a stock name, wait for the stock to come up, analyze the stock, type in the next stock name, wait again, and so on. This can be very time consuming. With a paid service, users can click through a list of charts in no time at all, without having to retype each stock's symbol.

Technical Analysis

A long, long time ago, in a place far, far away, financial analytical tools were designed by Ph.D. types using sophisticated software products. Those analytical tools were not available to an average person like you or me; only large financial companies could afford the computer hardware required to crunch the huge amounts of data. These days we can use these tools (discussed in detail in Chapter 4) on our little desktop computers.

The thing about these financial tools is this: While they may work at first, as more people begin using them on a regular basis their effect becomes neutralized. For example, pretend that you have a favorite restaurant that few people are aware of; it offers great food at cheap prices. You tell a friend, who tells a friend, and so on. Eventually, the demand for the food is so great that the owner raises the prices and has to hire additional cooks to help out. The new cooks may not cook as well as the owner. Pretty soon you have average food at high prices.

Some analytical tools still may be useful, especially if you use more than one or two of them at the same time. I found only one to be helpful with country fund analysis; I discuss it in Chapter 4. In the meantime, be aware that analytical tools are available and that the higher-priced software usually includes a greater variety and more advanced *indicators* and tools.

indicator data that provide information about or predict the overall health of the economy or the financial markets; examples are inflation, interest rates, employment, and volume.

Window on Wall Street's software includes a "chart expert" that explains what each analytical indicator can be used for and interprets your chart using an analytical tool. As you can imagine, this is a very useful function for new investors.

Actually, with professional software, you can select any number of indicators and the software automatically runs through the data and notes good opportunities. While I have not found these tools useful for analyzing country funds, I can see how they would be useful for regular company investments.

Another interesting feature of Window on Wall Street is the Profit "Tester." This feature allows you to take a certain amount of money and see how your investment would have performed over a certain time period using one or more analytical tools. Again, I can see how this would be useful for normal stock investments, but I have not found it useful for emerging markets. Furthermore, although various tools and strategies might have worked in the past, there is no guarantee that they will work in the future.

Portfolio Manager

Most online brokerage houses, investment software, and even the market pages of major newspapers' web sites offer free portfolio managers. (See Figure 3.8.) (www.Washingtonpost.com, for example, even has a very nice markets and investment site.) Basically, users type in key information, such as cash in and out, stock prices, and quantity of shares purchased and sold, and the portfolio manager keeps track of the value of the portfolio and individual security holdings. I have designed my own portfolio database using Microsoft Excel, and I also use Window on Wall Street's. Most online brokers also offer this service free of charge, but not all are updated in real time. Some portfolio managers will tell you tick by tick the value of your portfolio and how much you have made or lost on each stock.

Basic investment software may have numerous other features, such as the ability to bring in streaming financial or company news, create live tickers (a window that has stock prices moving across your screen, as you would see in Wall Street), and to design your own analytical tools.

PROFESSIONAL TOOLS

A true day trader who knows what he is doing (and I say "he" because, according to statistics, there are very few women who day trade—they

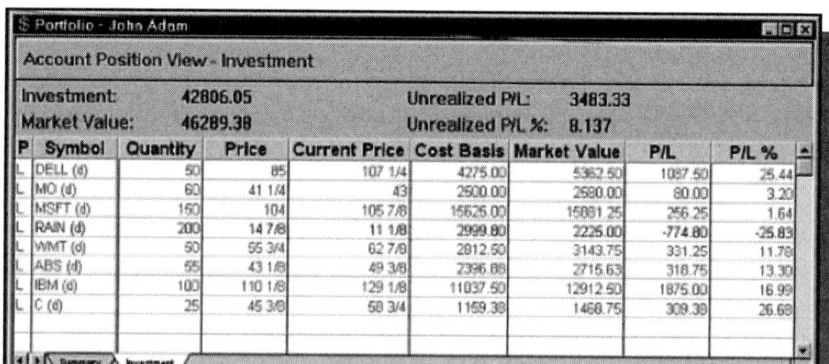

Portfolio - John Adam

Account Position View - Investment

Investment: 42806.05 Unrealized P/L: 3483.33

Market Value: 46289.38 Unrealized P/L %: 8.137

P	Symbol	Quantity	Price	Current Price	Cost Basis	Market Value	P/L	P/L %
L	DELL (d)	50	85	107 1/4	4275.00	5362.50	1087.50	25.44
L	MO (d)	60	41 1/4	43	2500.00	2580.00	80.00	3.20
L	MSFT (d)	150	104	105 7/8	15625.00	15881.25	256.25	1.64
L	RAIN (d)	200	14 7/8	11 1/8	2999.80	2225.00	-774.80	-25.83
L	WMT (d)	50	55 3/4	62 7/8	2812.50	3143.75	331.25	11.78
L	ABS (d)	55	43 1/8	49 3/8	2396.88	2715.63	318.75	13.30
L	IBM (d)	100	110 1/8	129 1/8	11037.50	12912.50	1875.00	16.99
L	C (d)	25	45 3/8	58 3/4	1159.38	1468.75	309.38	26.68

Summary Investment

FIGURE 3.8 Portfolio manager.

are too smart for that!) needs *very* powerful software. "Day trader" software products are different from the "Internet trader" series in that they have at least two additional features: (1) the Time and Sales Window and (2) Nasdaq Level 2 Capability.

The Time and Sales Window, shown in Figure 3.9, is a powerful execution tool. The figure presents a brief history of Microsoft (MSFT) stock transactions between 11:51:21 A.M. and 11:47:52 A.M. on January 7, 1997, trade by trade! Quite amazing, isn't it? Time and sales windows are for investors who require a lot more information than we do.

The other feature is the Nasdaq Level 2 window, as shown in Figure 3.10. This figure takes Amazon's stock information another step

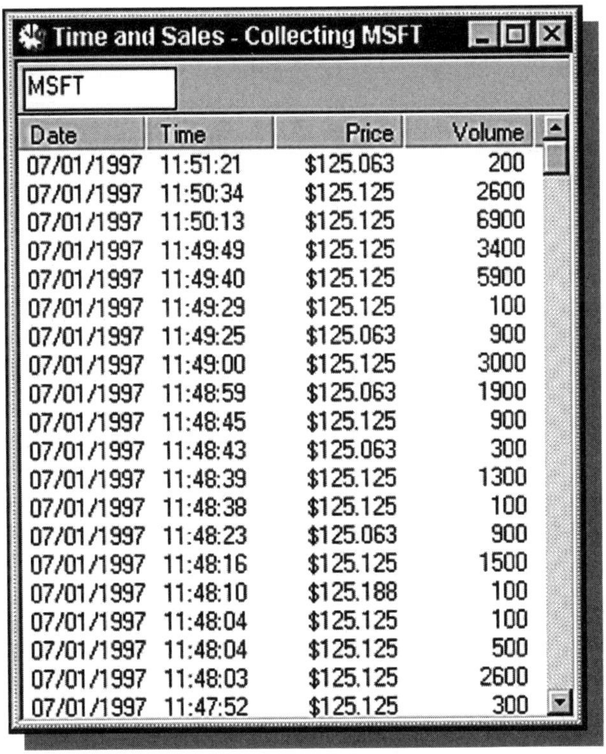

Date	Time	Price	Volume
07/01/1997	11:51:21	$125.063	200
07/01/1997	11:50:34	$125.125	2600
07/01/1997	11:50:13	$125.125	6900
07/01/1997	11:49:49	$125.125	3400
07/01/1997	11:49:40	$125.125	5900
07/01/1997	11:49:29	$125.125	100
07/01/1997	11:49:25	$125.063	900
07/01/1997	11:49:00	$125.125	3000
07/01/1997	11:48:59	$125.063	1900
07/01/1997	11:48:45	$125.125	900
07/01/1997	11:48:43	$125.063	300
07/01/1997	11:48:39	$125.125	1300
07/01/1997	11:48:38	$125.125	100
07/01/1997	11:48:23	$125.063	900
07/01/1997	11:48:16	$125.125	1500
07/01/1997	11:48:10	$125.188	100
07/01/1997	11:48:04	$125.125	100
07/01/1997	11:48:04	$125.125	500
07/01/1997	11:48:03	$125.125	2600
07/01/1997	11:47:52	$125.125	300

FIGURE 3.9 Time and sales window.

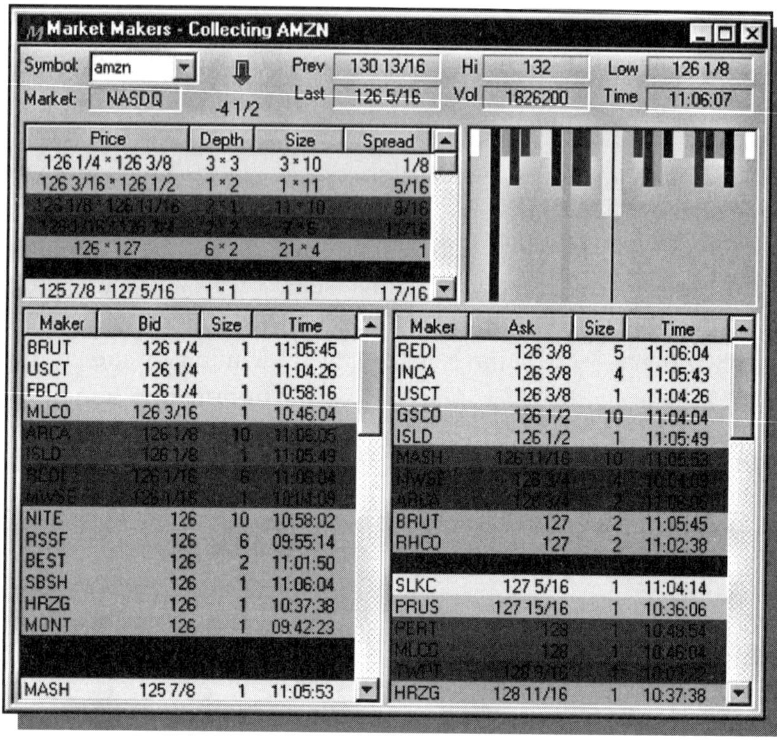

FIGURE 3.10 Nasdaq Level 2 window.

and actually tells you who is buying and selling the securities. This stuff does not concern us either.

FINANCIAL DATA OPTIONS

Investment tools are available both for nonprofessionals and for professionals. As far as I can tell, the free products and the services offered on many web sites have all of the features nonprofessionals need to buy, analyze, monitor, and sell single-country index funds.

Users can obtain data for free, or pay a monthly service charge for more timely data and more flexible and powerful analytical options.

Service charges vary by the amount of data required and how quickly the data are required. Some sites offer free real-time stock quotes, and others delay their quotes by 15 to 20 minutes.

I recommend moving up to the real-time, tick-by-tick service level once you have experimented a bit and are ready to commit your real, hard-earned cash. Again, prices vary by how many stocks you wish to track and the degree of information you required. If you are an amateur investor, the services offered by your online broker and Big Charts should be enough. The higher service levels are for serious day traders.

For those who are serious about investing in single-country closed-end funds, I recommend a software package that:

- ✔ Has flexible charting options
- ✔ Has a variety of basic analytical tools
- ✔ Can receive real-time data
- ✔ Has a window for monitoring real-time data
- ✔ Has an alarm feature
- ✔ Is cheap or free
- ✔ Allows end-of-day data retrieval

In Chapter 4 we will discuss some of the more common and useful analytical tools, and in Chapter 5 we will talk about how to buy and sell securities through an online broker. Chapters 3 through 5 can be viewed as a process:

- ✔ Data retrieval
- ✔ Data analysis
- ✔ Decision to purchase/sell
- ✔ Purchase/sell security

Chapter 4

Basic Stock Analysis

IN THE BEGINNING

Once we have the basic data (i.e., historical stock prices, volume, etc.) for country funds, we need to look at it from an analytical perspective, with the aim of predicting where the prices of the stocks that we are monitoring will move—up or down. I think most experts will agree that no one can predict the future, especially the future of stock markets. Once you actually start monitoring stocks and following markets, you will see that, on any particular day, while "experts" may predict that the market will move one way, the market often moves in the opposite direction. It's really a 50/50 shot!

Why, you may ask, should you spend your precious time analyzing data and markets? Although we really cannot predict where a stock will move, by using various indicators and other tools we can increase our chances of assessing good conditions to buy and sell *securities*. Chapter 5 discusses various investment strategies. But, for now, realize that understanding the basis of various investment indicators will give you an advantage over those who do not understand them. If you decide not to use the indicators, at least you will have a good reason for your decision.

security an investment instrument, other than an insurance policy or fixed annuity, issued by a corporation, government, or other organization that offers evidence of debt or equity.

CHART

Analysis begins with a chart. Earlier chapters provided many examples of basic charts. As you might have noticed, daily stock prices are presented as a range, not simply a point. Take a look at Figure 4.1, a one-week chart of AF (Argentina Fund).

As you can see, each day's price consists of a vertical line. The top of the vertical line is the highest price of the stock for the trading day; the lowest point of the line is the day's lowest price. (See Figure 4.2.) Thus, the price fluctuated during the day between these two points.

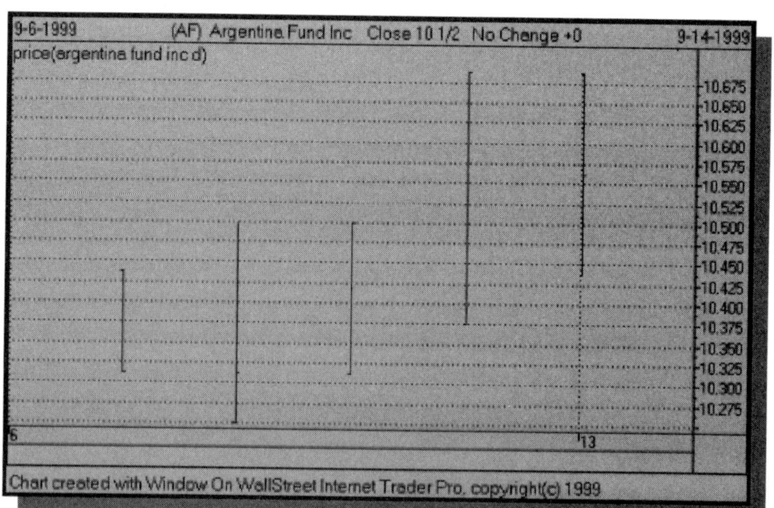

FIGURE 4.1 One-week chart of Argentina Fund (AF).

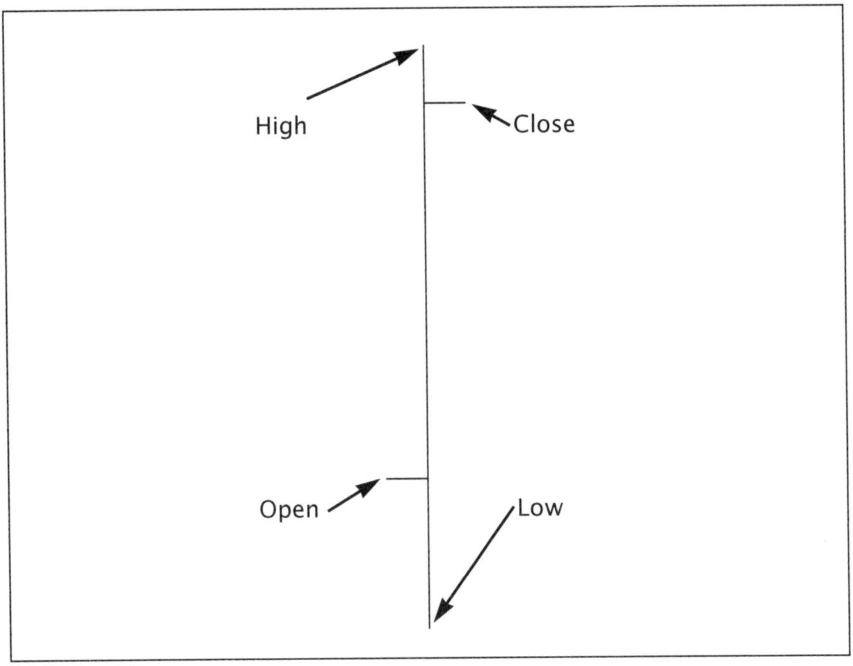

FIGURE 4.2 Example #1, an open/high/low/close bar.

The stock *opened* for the day at 9:30 A.M. at the small horizontal line on the left and *closed* at the upper horizontal line on the right.

Obviously, a stock can close at a price higher or lower than its open price; and the daily price range can vary for a variety of reasons. On a quiet trading day, for example, a stock's price range may be nar-

open the first price of a given security or commodity in a trading session.

close the price of the last transaction for a given security at the end of a given trading session.

row, indicating that the price did not change too much throughout the day. (Note, however, that this does not imply that the stock wasn't active during the day; the stock's volume might have been high, indicating a large number of shares were traded. The stock price, however, did not vary much throughout the day.)

Try not to read too much into the basic price chart, because the information is limited to the four variables: the open and close prices, and low and high points. This basic chart does not tell how or why the price actually moved during the day. Consider the following day's price movement, as shown in Figure 4.3.

This stock closed lower than it opened, and at some point during the day—we do not know when—it jumped up. It could have jumped up and stayed at a high price early on and only settled down later in the

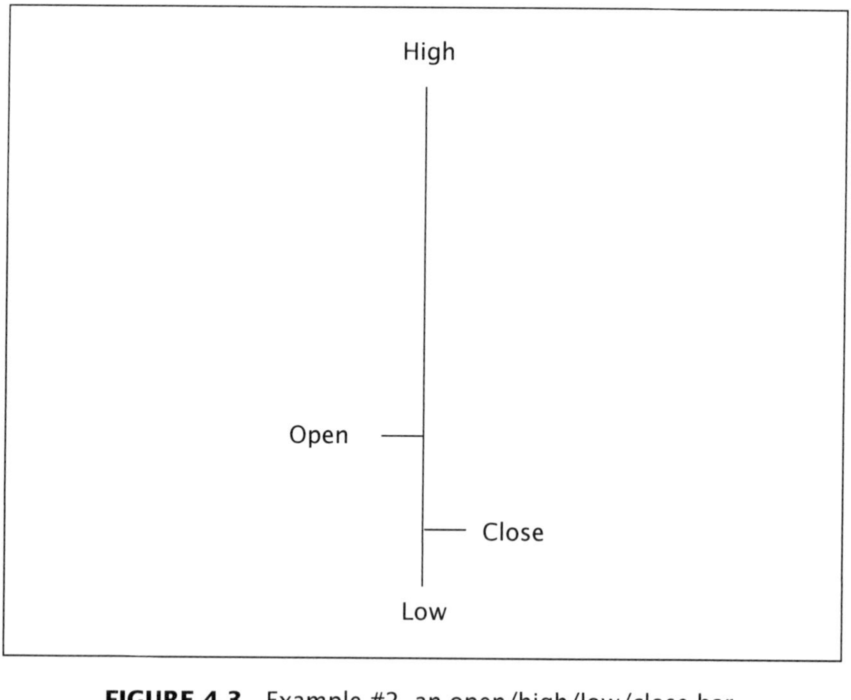

FIGURE 4.3 Example #2, an open/high/low/close bar.

day. Or the price might have increased gradually, topped around noon, and gradually landed before close.

TECHNICAL AND FUNDAMENTAL ANALYSIS

Stock analysis falls into two basic categories: (1) technical analysis and (2) fundamental analysis.

Technical Analysis

Technical analysis is based on the premise that a stock is the product of the free marketplace and that a stock's price is determined by competitive bidding. This is true. Technical analysts look at price, volume, and other factors to determine a stock's future behavior. Technical analysis is not concerned with what the company sells or the industry reports, or, in our case, with the political, social, or economic climate of a country, a region, and the world.

> **technical analysis** a method of evaluating securities by relying on the assumption that market data, such as charts of price, volume, and open interest, can help predict future (usually short-term) market trends. Unlike fundamental analysis, the technical analysis does not consider intrinsic value of the security.

Technical analysts believe that prices of stocks move in definite trends and that by using various technical indicators, they can predict these trends. They believe that a stock goes up only because there is a stronger interest in buying a stock than in selling it; buyers are willing to pay higher and higher prices to own the stock.

Later in the chapter I will introduce a number of the more popular technical indicators. I have found only one of them to be helpful for emerging market investments. As you may have realized, I am not a big fan of technical analysis as I do not believe we can predict the future, especially where countries are concerned. As I write this book, numerous international crises have popped up and dramatically affected the market. Earthquakes in Turkey and Taiwan (their stock markets dropped around 15 percent), an internal military crisis in Russia (my Russia fund dropped more than 20 percent in a week), yen and dollar issues, inflation and interest rate concerns in America, and on and on. Just today the Dow Jones is down over 2 percent because, and I quote from the *Washington Post*, "increasing concerns about the weakening dollar, the growing U.S. trade deficit and the upcoming earnings season."

Fundamental Analysis

Fundamental analysis is somewhat more useful for our country fund investments. For regular company stocks, the fundamental analysis approach relies on company reports, reporting publications by the *Securities and Exchange Commission (SEC)*, security analyst projections, and a host of other sources. Basically, one looks for fundamental information on the company to determine how the company will perform in the future.

> **fundamental analysis** a method of security valuation that involves examining the company's financials and operations, especially sales, earnings, growth potential, assets, debt, management, products, and competition.

As I mentioned earlier, large investment companies actually send their analysts and managers to companies to visit with management. Individual investors like you or me can quickly and easily calculate a host of valuable financial ratios derived from a relatively small (12 to 15) number of fundamental facts (e.g., sales, dividends, earnings, cash,

> **Securities and Exchange Commission (SEC)** the primary federal regulatory agency for the securities industry, whose responsibility it is to promote full disclosure and to protect investors against fraudulent and manipulative practices in the securities markets.

liabilities) about a company. Typically this information is useful only when compared with data from similar companies.

> **liability** a financial obligation, debt, claim, or potential loss.

For closed-end country funds, fundamental analysis is broader, and includes analyzing global, regional, and country political, economic, and social issues. Fundamental information on emerging market countries was presented in Chapter 2.

Next we explore the various indicators that can be used for stock analysis. Again, most will not be terribly useful for our country funds, but you still should have a basic understanding of their strengths and weaknesses. Some may prove helpful for your particular investment style.

GENERIC INDICATORS

Trendlines

A *trendline* is the most basic tool available, and yet I find it one of the most powerful. A trendline is simply a straight line that connects a series of security prices.

There are three trendline types:

1. *Support trendline*—placed along the bottom of a price movement
2. *Resistance trendline*—placed along the top of a price movement
3. *Channel trendline*—placed in between support and resistance trendlines, interpreted as a trading range

trendline technical analysis formation created by drawing a line connecting a series of descending tops, descending bottoms, ascending tops, or ascending bottoms.

support in technical analysis, a price level that a security has had difficulty falling below.

resistance inability of a stock to rise above a certain price (its resistance level).

As an example, Figure 4.4 presents a few support trendlines for the Spain Fund. As you can see, the stock's price tends to have support around 14.5—it bounces down and back up around this line. Commonly, when a stock breaks through its support line, its pattern may be broken, and it may continue downward to a new level.

Similarly, the resistance trendline seems to be a ceiling that keeps the price from moving upward. Often, once this line is broken through, the stock will climb to a new level. Figure 4.5 provides examples of re-

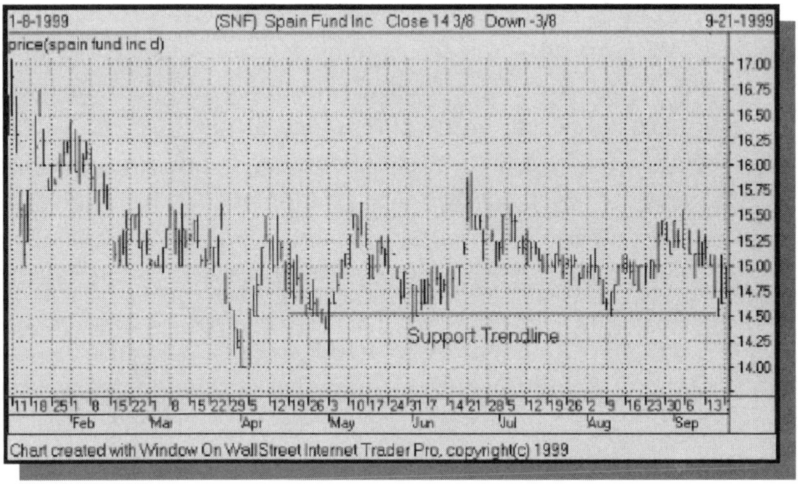

FIGURE 4.4 Trendlines.

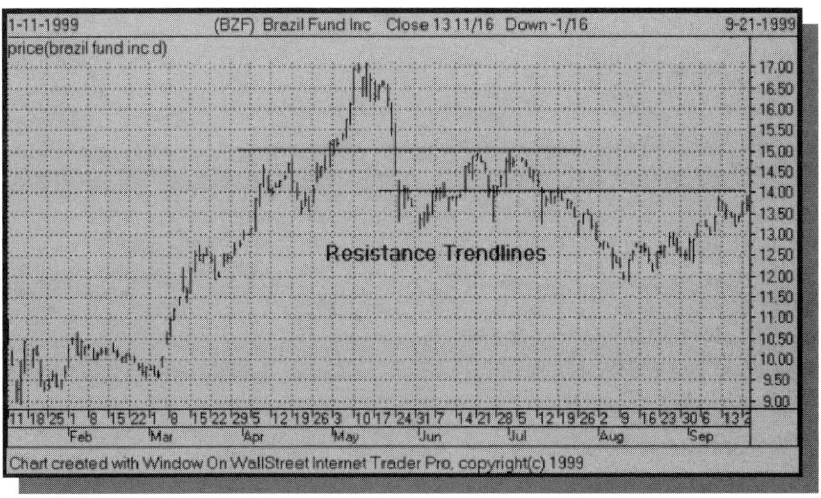

FIGURE 4.5 Resistance trendlines.

sistance trendlines. The resistance levels are not as clean as the support lines were in Figure 4.4—BZF seems to have two resistance trendlines, one around 14 and the other around 15—but they are still quite useful.

Trendlines are based on the psychology of investors. As you can see from Figure 4.6, resistance and support levels often hover around whole numbers. There is no technical or fundamental basis for this—people just like to buy and sell around these points. In general, the length of time the trendline has persisted without being penetrated indicates the strength of the line.

For example, if I bought AOL at 100, I might set a goal to sell at 105, or 110, or 120. But it would be unlikely that I would set a goal to sell at 117.

Arcs and Fans

There are tons of odd-sounding instruments, based on lines and arcs and angles, that you may wish to play with. These are not fundamental or technical indicators but just various "trendlines" that some investors have found helpful.

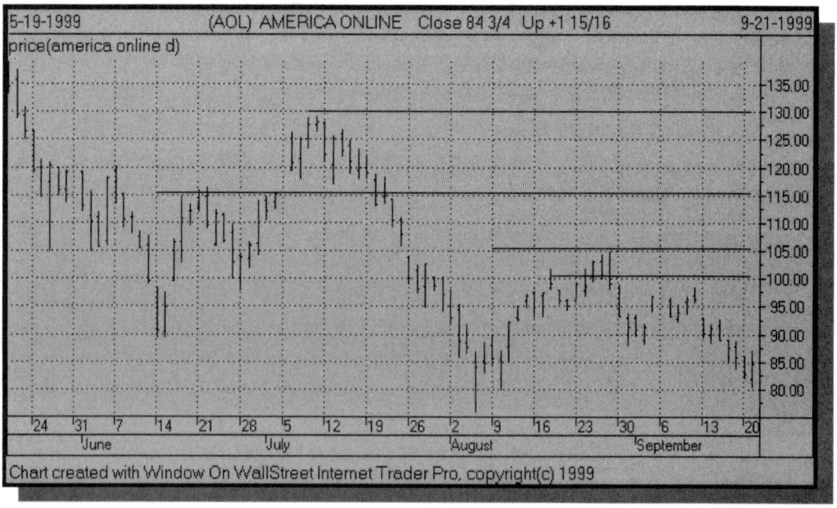

FIGURE 4.6 Resistance trendlines.

Figure 4.7 is an example of one, the Fibonacci arcs. I selected a major low and high point, and my computer program did the rest: three arcs at intervals of 38.2, 50.0, and 61.8 percent. Apparently, the arcs project into the future. Theoretically, the points at which the arcs intersect with the price movement may represent areas of support or resistance.

The Window on Wall Street program includes the following trendline features, none of which have been useful in my country fund analysis: Fibonacci arcs, Fibonacci fans, Fibonacci time zones, Andrew's pitchfork, cycle lines, Gann angles, Gann retracement, and quadrant lines.

TECHNICAL INDICATORS

Technical indicators are used in technical analysis to identify and interpret trends in price movements. In general, technical indicators can be classified into two categories:

1. *Trend-following indicators* often are useful in identifying a change in a trend *after* it has occurred. They work well when the trends identified are significant. The moving average, discussed in the next section, is an example of a trend-following indicator.

2. *Oscillators* are useful when price movements are not strongly trending and may be moving horizontally up and down for a given period of time. For the later part of 1998 and first half of 1999, most of my trading occurred during these up and down cycles. I used the commodity channel index, discussed below, to help with my investment decisions during this period. Oscillator indicators also may be used to signal overbought or oversold conditions in a trending movement.

Moving Averages

Because most technical indicators are not designed actually to predict the future (which would be hard to do anyway), they are not very use-

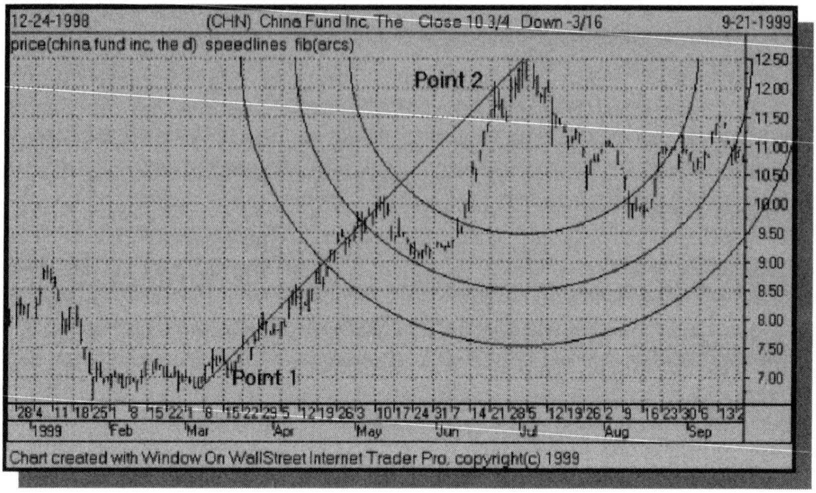

FIGURE 4.7 Chart displaying use of Fibonacci arcs.

ful for country fund investing. However, the *moving average* function can be informative, at the very least.

The moving average is one of the more popular trend-following indicators used in technical analysis. Basically, it is used to smooth out variations in a plot.

The solid line in Figure 4.8 is the moving average. At each point along the plot, the numerical average of the previous number of periods (typically, 30 days, but you can select any number of periods for the equation) is calculated and drawn. In effect, the moving average gives another perspective of the current price of a stock by shaving off major highs and lows during the period.

moving average a technical analysis term meaning the average price of a security over a specified time period. Used in order to spot pricing trends by flattening out large fluctuations.

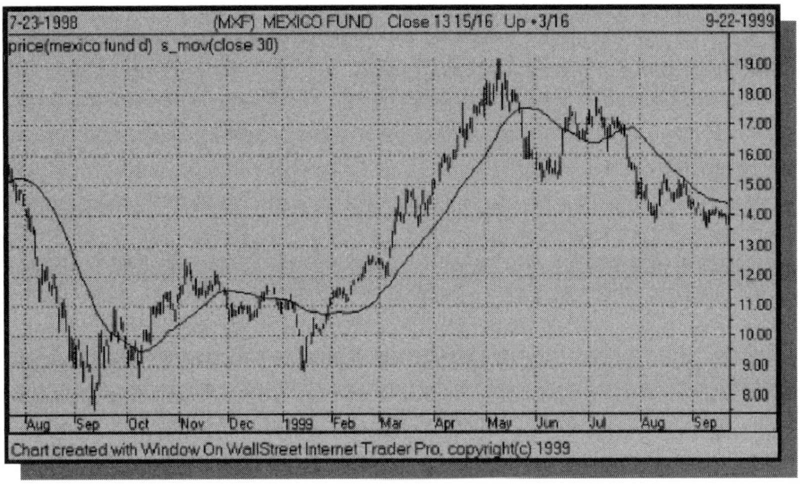

FIGURE 4.8 Example of a simple moving average.

What can the moving average be used for? If the real price movement is significantly above the moving average line, this may indicate that the stock is due for a downturn. The converse is also true—trading significantly below the moving average may indicate that a stock is ready to move up.

Figure 4.8 shows us that the use of the moving average as a prediction does work some of the time. However, referring to Figure 4.8 of MXF during the three-month period March–May 1999, the price rose dramatically. If you relied on the moving average as a predictor of future price movements, you probably would have sold out much before the peak.

There are three basic types of moving averages:

1. The *simple moving average* is calculated by adding the prices for a number of periods and dividing by the number of periods. While this method is fairly effective, its one disadvantage is that it gives equal weight to each period's price, rather than weighing the actions of recent periods more.

2. The *exponential moving average* gives more weight to recent prices and ever decreasing weight to older data. This makes more sense, since market conditions change everyday, and more recent developments obviously will have a greater effect on current and future price developments. Interestingly, unlike the other two types of averages, when calculating exponential moving averages the older data never go away.

3. The *weighted moving average* gives each period's price a weight based on its age—older periods are given a weight of 1, and the weight increases by 1 until the final period is reached.

It is obvious on Figure 4.9 that the three types of moving averages, although different in how they are calculated, are actually quite similar in movement.

Price Oscillator

The price oscillator, a technical indicator based on moving averages, is calculated using the differences between two moving averages of the price. It can be calculated in dollars or as a percentage. (See Figure 4.10.)

FIGURE 4.9 Three types of moving averages.

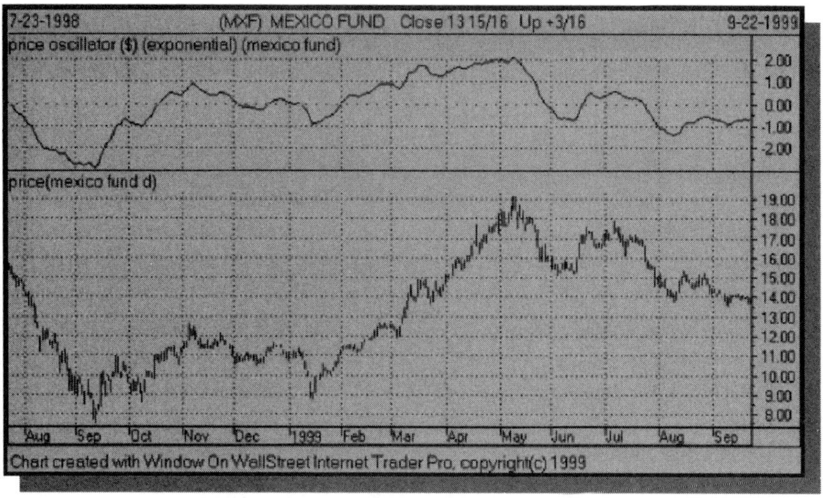

FIGURE 4.10 Example of the price oscillator.

Theoretically, as the price oscillator line moves down and crosses the zero mark, it is a good time to buy; when the line moves upward through the zero mark, it is a good time to sell.

Moving average crossover systems like the price oscillator were some of the first technical indicators designed to analyze stock market data. As computers entered into the picture, and as they became more advanced, so did the indicators designed by financial specialists. Thus, I would not rely on the price oscillator indicator too much when making investment decisions.

Commodity Channel Index

The commodity channel index is an example of a more sophisticated technical indicator and is the only one that I use on a daily basis. By "use," I mean glance at occasionally; it is often an adequate predictor of future price movements. I would never use it as my sole reason for an investment decision, however. Figure 4.11 is a chart of the Mexico

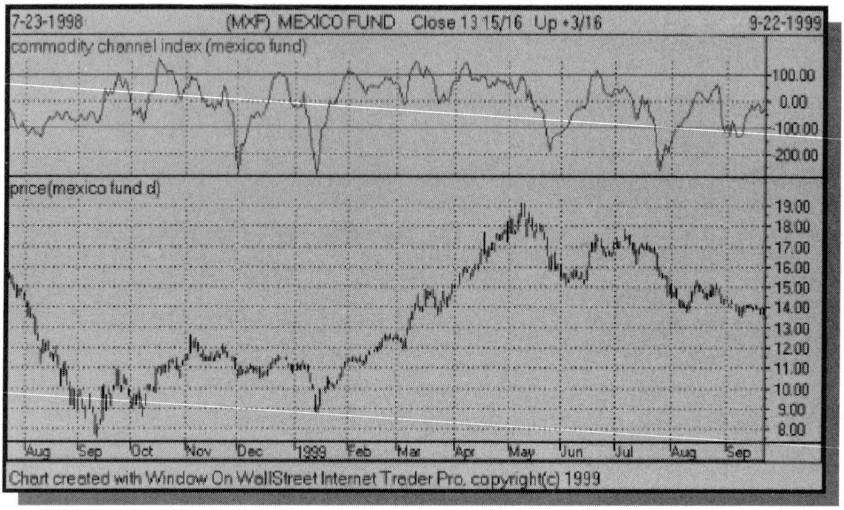

FIGURE 4.11 Example of a commodity channel index.

Fund from August 1998 through September 1999. The commodity channel index is displayed in the upper window.

The commodity price index is a price movement indicator that creates an index similar to a statistical standard score measuring the price exclusions from the mean price as a standard variation. The mean price of a security is compared to the security's average mean price over a given period of time.

This all is rather complicated. What matters is that, out of all of the indicators I tested on country funds, the commodity channel indicator actually works (some of the time).

This indicator helps determine when a *cyclical* trend exists in a price. Normally, the index will remain in the –100 to +100 range, which means that the price is following its anticipated cyclicality. When the index goes outside of this range, a new trend may be emerging; movements beyond these values are supposed to be nonrandom and create new trading opportunities.

The trading rules are as follows:

- ✔ When the index (the flowing line) rises *above* the 100 mark, it may signal a good time to sell.
- ✔ When the index crosses *below* the –100 line, it may be a good time to buy.

> **cyclical** something that happens periodically, that is, on a regular basis.

Chapter 5 presents my investment philosophy in more detail and explains how I utilize the commodity channel index.

The story of how I discovered that this index often works for country funds is interesting. When I first acquired my investment software, I tested each indicator (100 or so) on a representative sample of country funds. Initially a few indicators seemed to be good predictors. I tested each over numerous time ranges with varying market conditions, such as *bear markets* and bull markets; markets with huge swings upward and downward (could the indicators predict a crash, for example); and just average periods where not much is happening (a period between a bear or bull market). I was very interested to see whether any indicator would have predicted the world stock market downturn of 1994.

> **bear market** a prolonged period of falling prices, usually by 20 percent or more, accompanied by widespread pessimism.

At first, many of the indicators worked, and I was ecstatic. I did not know anyone who actively traded country funds on a regular basis, and since this type of sophisticated software had become available in retail stores only recently, I thought I might have discovered a pot of gold.

Then reality set in: These indicators were merely *following* the market, not *predicting* it. They really were not even doing a good job *indicating*. The commodity channel index, on the other hand, seemed to do a bit of predicting.

Two popular indicators that I originally had hope in were the moving average convergence divergence and the money flow index.

MACD

The moving average convergence divergence (MACD) is an oscillator based on the spread difference between two exponential moving averages of the closing price. The difference between these 12-period and 26-period moving averages is then smoothed by a 9-period exponential moving average. This is called the signal line.

The solid line on Figure 4.12 is the MACD line. The dotted line is the trigger line. When the MACD line is negative and below the trigger line, and then moves back above the trigger line, theoretically this may be a good time to buy. Likewise, when the MACD line is positive and above the trigger line, and moves back below the trigger line, this may be a good time to sell or enter a short position.

As you can see in Figure 4.12, there are four periods during which the MACD makes a big drop below the trigger line, signaling a good time to buy. And, look, shortly after, the stock's price increases, as shown in Figure 4.13.

Upon closer inspection, you will see that the MACD *follows* the price and thus really does not give any indication of future price movements. From the price movement shown in Figure 4.13, it would indeed seem like a good time to buy as the stock price dropped so much recently. It is a self-fulfilling prophecy!

Now look at Figure 4.14. If you purchased stock when they suggested (as the MACD, in negative territory, comes up from a dip and crosses the signal line), you would have purchased at a peak and before a downturn. This is a not good thing!

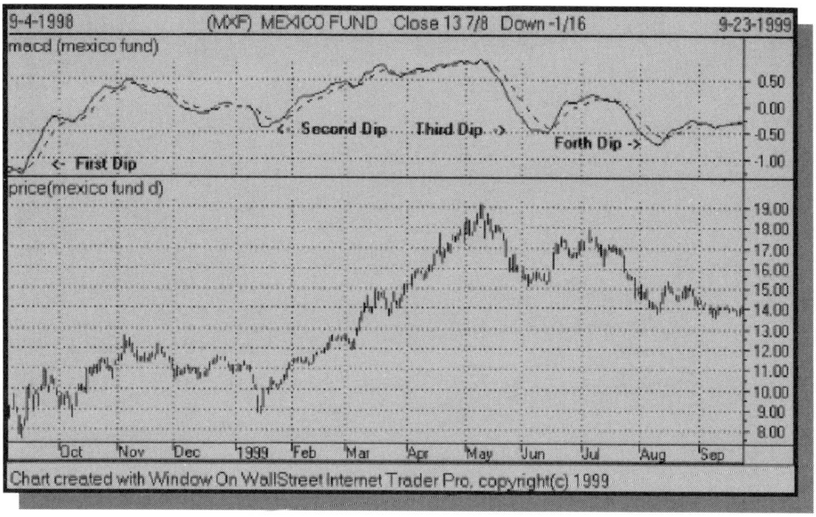

FIGURE 4.12 Example of the moving average convergence divergence (MACD).

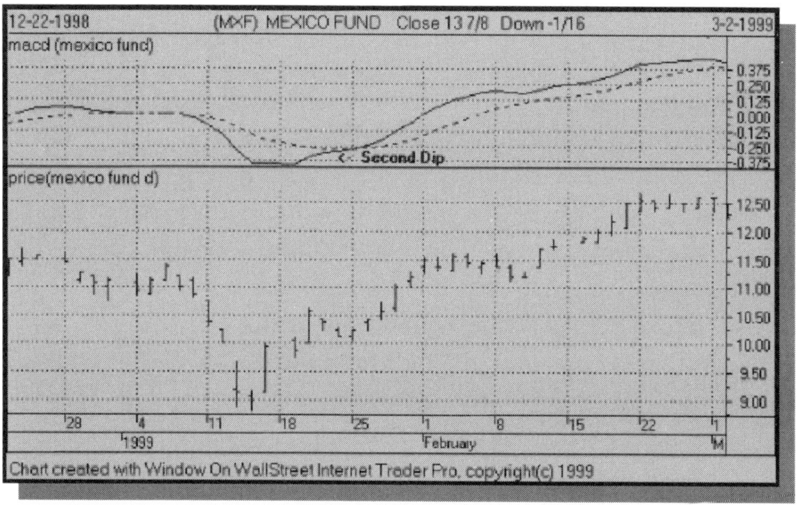

FIGURE 4.13 A closer look at the MACD.

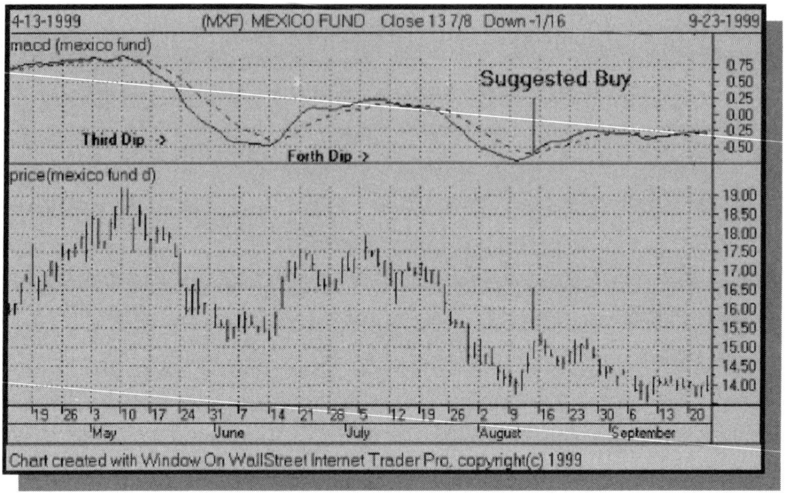

FIGURE 4.14 The failing of the MACD.

Money Flow Index

The money flow index is a volume weighted version of the relative strength index, another commonly used technical indicator. This indicator takes into account volume and thus is based on activity, not simply on price movements.

When I first viewed the money flow index on a chart, I was impressed; the formula seemed to work. If the index is below the 20 mark, the model suggests that it is a good time to buy; and if the index line rises above 80, it may be a good time to sell. Study Figure 4.15 for a while and see if you think the indicator works.

In June/July of 1997, the indicator warned us to sell. This was a good thing because the market soon dropped by more than 50 percent. However, note that in mid-1998 and thereafter, the indicator suggested that we sell five times. If we sold the first four times the money flow index crossed the 80 line, we would have lost out on a major upward climb.

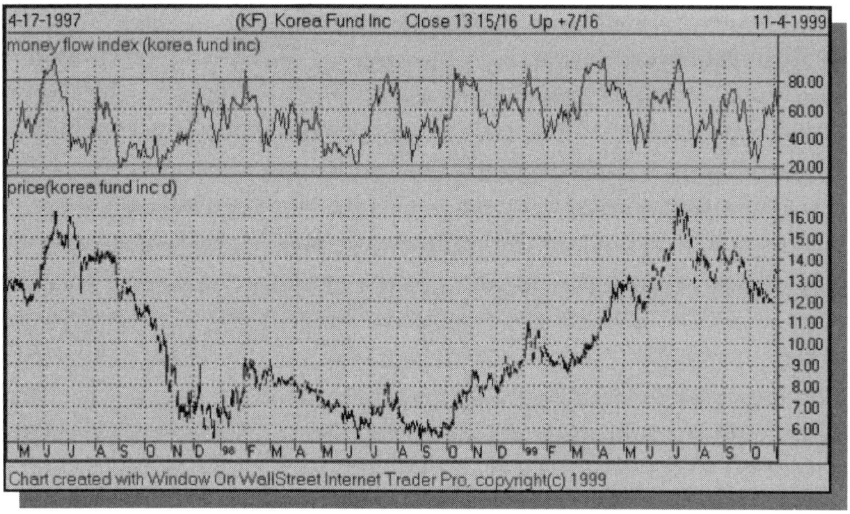

FIGURE 4.15 Example of the money flow index.

Beta

Beta is an indicator that you may find useful. Similar to the relative strength index, beta calculates the relative performance of one security to another. A value greater than 1 is a possible sign that the first security is more volatile than the second. Beta is often used in rating the volatility of stocks relative to an index like the Dow Jones Average.

beta a quantitative measure of the volatility of a given stock, mutual fund, or portfolio, relative to the overall market, usually the Standard & Poor's (S&P) 500. Specifically, the performance the stock, fund, or portfolio has experienced in the last five years as the S&P moved 1 percent up or down. A beta above 1 is more volatile than the overall market, while a beta below 1 is less volatile.

Figure 4.16 presents the Brazil Fund in the bottom panel, the Dow Jones Industrial Average in the middle, and Brazil Fund's beta in the top pane; the top pane compares the Brazil Fund's price line to the Dow. In general, the fund tends to be more choppy in its movements—showing more dramatic ups and downs than the Dow. This is volatility. Beta jumps above 1 frequently, often hitting 2 or 3, signaling a high volatility. This is a good thing for us, because it means that often we can pick up shares of Brazil at good prices when it makes its frequent dips. American markets are usually steadier, and do not have these significant price movements.

FUNDAMENTAL INDICATORS

As you have seen, technical analysis is very monolithic in that it tries to forecast the future price of a stock based on the statistical interpretation of the supply and demand of that stock and how that affects its price; technical analysts use mathematical indicators to forecast the

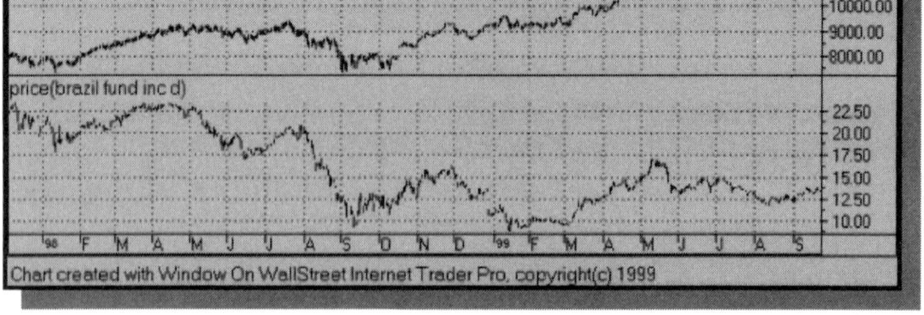

FIGURE 4.16 Example of the use of beta.

timing of price trends in the market. This sounds more like a crap shoot than an investment strategy.

Fundamental analysis, on the other hand, attempts to forecast the future value of a stock by analyzing the company's current and historical financial strength based more on personal measures, such as sales, earnings, liabilities, assets, and dividends. Although there are many other "fundamental" measures, such as the strength of a company's management team and the quality of the product, data for sales, earnings, and dividends are readily available for analysis with investment software. Fundamental indicators include:

✔ *Cumulative dividend equity:* Allows you to see the gross cumulative sum of dividend equity earned for a block of shares you own. (Some country funds do pay out dividends, by the way.)

✔ *Current dividend yield:* Plots the percentage of the current dividend relative to the current price. This enables the stockholder not to have to depend on price change to recoup his or her investment.

✔ *Dividends:* Payments designated by a corporation's board of directors to be distributed to shareholders on a pro rata basis. These payments are a share of company profits disbursed for various reasons: to minimize corporate taxes, increase investor loyalty, or create a greater interest among investors. By definition, dividend history is not actually an indicator, but historical dividend information can be a useful gauge of a company's long-term profitability.

✔ *Earnings per share:* Possibly the most commonly used ratio. EPS measures how a company's net earnings are spread across the total number of common stock shares issued. Usually EPS is reported on a quarterly basis.

Just like changes in price data, changes in EPS over time may indicate the future price movement of a stock. As companies' earnings are cyclical in nature, the current quarter's EPS can be compared to the same quarter of the previous year. Solid EPS growth may indicate a stock poised for increase.

✔ *Price/earnings (P/E) ratio:* This is the current market price of a security divided by some measure of earnings per share. A stock with a lower P/E ratio indicates that the stock is more desirable, as the stock price is low compared with the earnings.

> **price/earnings (P/E) ratio** the most common measure of how expensive a stock is; equal to a stock's capitalization divided by its after-tax earnings over a 12-month period.

A country fund is obviously not a company and thus does not have "earnings" and "dividends" per se. Fundamental indicators available in the analysis software will not be of much help to us.

Fundamental measures for countries are similar to those for companies—they are just on a larger scale. A country's GDP, or even imports/exports, could be compared to a company's sales; the political leadership to a management team; the social environment and culture to corporate culture; and so on. Unfortunately, at this time, we cannot download this important fundamental data for use with chart analysis. But we certainly can pick up this information daily in the press (or from Chapter 2 in this book), along with other critical information, such as major world crises, inflation and interest rates, and the general investment mood (bull/bear, etc.).

Chapter 5

Investment Strategies and Other Important Stuff

READY, SET, GO!

By now you should have a good understanding of the countries and their funds that you will soon invest in and have purchased useful yet reasonably priced stock investment software. The next steps are:

- ✔ Gathering relevant information
- ✔ Developing a personal investment strategy
- ✔ Making purchase decisions
- ✔ Selecting an online broker
- ✔ Purchasing stock through an online broker

This is a very exciting chapter because you will begin to develop your own investment strategy. I will help by walking you through my basic strategies and my daily investment routines.

We will look at four time frame models that require different strategies to make profitable investments:

1. Day trading
2. Short-term trading/investing
3. Medium-term investing
4. Long-term investing

And, we will investigate *risk*—what it means to you, in terms of your tolerance levels and goals—and methods to decrease overall risk as much as possible with each of the four investment methods listed above.

risk the quantifiable likelihood of loss or less-than-expected returns.

We also will cover advice and a number of rules and laws. These tips are quite important—whether you follow them or not will determine if you succeed or fail as an investor.

1. Do your homework.
2. Be careful whom you listen to (except me, of course).
3. Start out small to test the waters.
4. Recheck all orders before your final click.
5. Diversify, diversify, diversify.
6. Day trading does not work.
7. In general, invest for the long term.
8. Buy low, sell high.
9. Leveraging can make you rich—or poor.

10. Do not freak out—controlling your emotions can make or break you.
11. Do not look back once you sell.

Although I compiled this list from my own investment strategies and experiences, few successful investors would disagree with its points.

And, in Chapter 6, I will introduce you to a variety of online brokers and take you through the steps of selecting one, setting up an online account, and making stock purchases and sales through your new broker.

YOUR FIRST STEPS

The first thing you should do, now that you have a complete list of the country funds and their symbols and stock analysis software, is to download historical data for each of the funds. Once you have done so, refer back to the country information in Chapter 2 and go through each of the charts on your computer.

It is interesting to compare price movements from country to country, region to region, looking for common trends. Since you probably worked very hard to earn the money you are about to invest, it is in your best interest to spend sufficient time understanding how this all works.

RULE #1: Do Your Homework

Although investing in country funds is not very difficult, learning about the specific funds, your new software, and how to place orders online does take a good deal of initial time up front. Some people do not want to learn about the countries they are going to invest in—they want to rely solely on the charts. If that is the case with you, maybe country funds are not the right investment vehicle for you; I would stick to Nasdaq stocks, if I were you, as they are more technical and fundamental-analysis friendly.

Take time to understand each country and each chart so you understand the personality of each. Doing so will not only be beneficial to your returns, but it will make the process a lot more fun. Each time you place an order, you can visually imagine the country you are investing in, its people, culture, industries, and companies. Unlike many other stocks, these actually have a great deal of flavor and character. You are investing in countries and the people who live in the countries—not in charts and statistics.

My investment routine includes 30 to 60 minutes in the morning to read a major newspaper (I use www.Washingtonpost.com) or two and a few other sites with financial information (i.e., cnnfn.com; Amazon.com's Personal Finance section has a number of great links to popular and respected sites). I also spend time monitoring the market during the day during very active periods.

When the U.S. market closes, I often read the market summary on www.cnnfn.com's front page. I just like to hear what the word on the street is regarding the day's market performance. Shortly after the market closes, my computer automatically downloads chart information on my country funds for analysis.

During end-of-day analysis, I click through the 50 or so charts that I regularly monitor, looking for major downward movements and stocks hitting their support and resistance lines. This process does not take long, as it is easy to spot these notable dips and drops. If there is a stock I wish to purchase, I may print out the chart and select a price I would like to buy at tomorrow. I also take a look at the charts of funds in my portfolio to see how they are doing.

End-of-day analysis takes about 15 minutes or so. When you go through your first analysis of each country fund chart, try to look into major periods of ups and downs to discover underlying causes of these major movements. Compare various charts with one another to see if any seem to move together or follow American markets. You will find that most funds are affected in some way by what happens in the United States.

RULE #2: Be Careful Whom You Listen To

In Chapter 1, I told how I learned firsthand how the big financial companies have some degree of control over the market. Don't get me wrong; I don't think they have complete control over the markets. I am not a conspiracy theorist. But I do know that they have huge war chests, and these unbelievable sums of money can influence market movements. Also, the heads of many of these firms belong to the same clubs and groups and share information that we are not privy too.

So, first, be careful whom you listen to because many of these companies have a strong influence over the media, either because the media are interested in what these big players have to say or because they own part of the media. Large financial groups often leak information or take particular stances on issues to influence the market to their advantage.

Second, the media need news, and when there is no news, they make non-news news. As I mentioned many times, no one can predict the future, including where a stock or stock market will move next. Just because you read a report from a reputable source does not mean that the information is fact. I am sure there are just as many other experts who believe the opposite.

You are investing in the world—literally. What this means is that you must take in as much information as possible, on both a macro- and a microlevel (global and country level). You must be objective, unemotional, and future oriented. Listen to everyone's perspective with an open mind, realizing that each opinion is just one of many.

RULE #3: Start Out Small

A very wise rule indeed! At first, you may wish to use fake dollars, say $10,000 or so, to play with and test various strategies. I recommend that you test the waters in three phases:

1. Experiment with various approaches on historical data over various periods of time. The key here is to hide future historical data from yourself so you can see how the different strategies work. The Window on Wall Street software I use has a program that tests various indicators automatically, individually or in groups. All of the indicators I tried on country funds with this program actually lost money.

So you should manually apply each indicator to a selection of country fund charts (diversified by region) and see if any of the indicators seem to work. If and when you have found a few with good prospects, test them out over a historical time period to see if they are good predictors of future prices. Doing so may take some time because you must pretend you are actually investing on a daily basis, purchasing and selling stock as if it were in the present.

I have found that testing your theories and indicators weekly does not work. You must make your experiments as similar to real-time investing as possible. If you cut corners in your modeling phase, your future investment strategy will most certainly be limited in its power and accuracy.

Again, success depends on you and you alone; beware of investment advisors, experts, and software as they all have major limitations.

2. Once you feel comfortable with your investment strategy and have a good understanding of country funds and investment tools, try out your theories on real-time data, but still using fake money.

If you are not in a rush, I suggest you take six months to experiment during this phase.

3. The third trial phase is where you use your real money—but not too much of it, for heavens sake! Don't get cocky because you have had great success during the first two phases. Market conditions change all the time, and you still may need more training. Take another six months or so, gradually increasing your portfolio. If your name doesn't end with "Trump," I suggest starting with $3,000 to $5,000, investing $1,000 or so at a time. At this stage, you may have between three and six stocks in your portfolio.

If the world markets are near bottom when you start, however, I advise jumping in and making some long-term buys. Put those investments aside while you play with a lesser amount. Early in the new decade will be a rare and ideal time to invest in country funds for long-term positions—I don't let this opportunity slide!

RULE #4: Recheck All Orders

Many people lose some money early in their investment career by not being careful when placing orders and not rechecking their entries. When you purchase or sell stock through an online broker, you must type in a lot of detailed information. Inaccurate data could cost you a lot of money. You could buy or sell a different quantity of shares from what you intended, place an order to buy or sell at a significantly different price from what you intended, or possibly trade the wrong security.

It is very easy to get caught up in the crazed rush when markets and prices are moving rapidly. Your adrenaline will have your heart and brain racing. This is okay and can even be fun, but you still must learn to control your emotions and take sufficient time to make intelligent, wise, and accurate investment decisions—especially when placing orders.

In the next chapter I take you through the steps of buying and selling stock through an online broker. But for now, keep in mind that you should take your time and check and double check all orders you place. By "double check," I mean actually look at each and every figure that you input, check your order type (limit, market, etc.), recalculate shares and costs, and check the going market price, first on the original input screen and again on the confirmation screen.

BASIC TIME STRATEGIES

There are an infinite number of stock investment strategies. I think the best way to categorize them is by your time horizon: Do you like to spend most of your time each day in front of your computer stressed out investing in stocks, do you place occasional orders and sit back and let your portfolio ride for a few years or more—or are you somewhere in between the two?

I have utilized all four approaches over time depending on market conditions, but short- to medium-term trading has been my norm. In early 2000 my strategy is changing more to buy and hold. As I mentioned in Chapter 1, as Asia and other parts of the world come out of a recession, most emerging markets should gradually rise to their previous highs—and I do not want to miss out on that!

RULE #5: Diversify

Chapter 1 stated that diversification is a good reason to invest in emerging markets. Experts agree that people should have a healthy mix (up to 50 percent) invested in foreign instruments. Diversification also includes the *type* of financial instruments, such as stocks, bonds, real estate, cash, gold, and jewelry.

A major element of diversification for global investors is regional and country diversification. Don't put all of your eggs in one basket: Spread your investment capital around the world. Yes, it is okay to have a regional preference, and to put a disproportionate amount in that region. I prefer Asia, for example. But I also invest quite regularly in South America and other regions. If one region hits a gloomy period, whether economic, political, or social, your entire portfolio will not be affected if you are diversified.

Which time strategy you select really will depend on the time you have available, your tolerance for risk, and, again, market conditions. Let's go through each strategy now so you can get a better idea how you want to invest.

Day Trading

Day trading is when a person buys and sells shares of stock during a day and sells off the complete portfolio by the close of the day; no stock is carried over to the next day, only cash. Obviously, day trading is a full-time job.

There has been a lot of controversy over day trading recently, and for good reason. First, understand that day trading is not investing. Investing is where you *invest* in something—in this case, companies. You buy stock in a company when you believe that it is strong and has a good future; and you want a piece of its success. I suppose people selling options are also investing in a way—many people believe that a company will *not* perform well, and will invest in its downfall. Regardless, *investing* in companies is more medium to long term, as it usually takes time for a company to grow and its stock value to increase sufficiently.

Day trading is not investing because day traders usually do not know that much about the companies they are buying in to. Day traders follow hot leads in the news and rely on technical indicators. They try to buy stock as momentum rises and get out quickly before it falls. Day trading is, in effect, gambling; day traders are professional gamblers!

RULE #6: Day Trading Does Not Work

Theoretically day traders can make money by placing many, many trades during a day, trying to make a small profit from each. I've heard day traders say that their goal is to make as little as one-sixteenth on a trade and then get out. They believe that these small profits add up. I don't think so, however.

Say day traders play with $50,000 during a given day and buy stock in $5,000 lots, allowing for 10 active trades at a given time. If the traders buy a stock trading at 50 and sells it within the hour at $50^1/_4$, they would make $10 (after taking out a very generous $15 for broker fees; limit orders would cost more). I suppose, if they were lucky, they might make 10 to 20 of these trades during a day, making $100 to $200 a day. In a month, that would be $2,000 to $4,000. I suppose that is not a bad living, but this model assumes that, out of 10 to 20 daily trades, the gamblers—I mean traders—did not have any losing transactions. Good luck!

Very few day traders make money; some reports state that 90 percent of day traders lose money. Out of that 10 percent who actually make money, how many actually make enough to make a decent living? Say a day trader starts out with $30,000 to play with. Let's pretend that he is one of the lucky 10 percent, and actually makes money. Let's be generous and give him a 100 percent return, or $30,000 over a year, after transaction costs. After taxes, he is left with $20,000 or so. Not much to live on!

There are times, however, that you may see an opportunity to make a quick buck. Every now and then a country fund will drop 10 to 15 percent in one day, for one reason or another. For example, when Turkey had a major earthquake in mid-August of 1999, TKF's price sank in a few days, as shown in Figure 5.1.

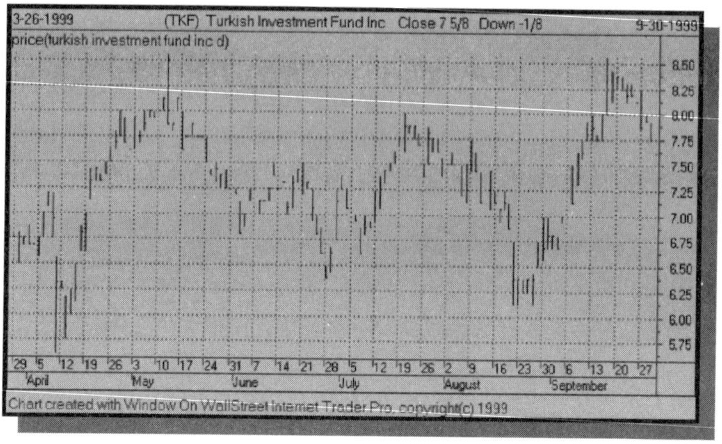

FIGURE 5.1 Earthquake in August affects the Turkish market.

Here I bought in around $6^1/_4$, and sold when it reached its resistance line around $7^3/_4$. If I held onto the stock for another week, I would have made a lot more money—but you cannot predict these things. My strategy is to stick to the original plan. Greed will put you in the poorhouse!

Every day, throughout the day, I check my entire list of country funds to monitor overall percentage gains and losses to see if there are any good opportunities like this. If a stock drops significantly, as TKF did, I may purchase it and hold it for a day or so, until it makes 5 to 15 percent, depending on my chart analysis.

But this really is not day trading per se since I am not pressured to dump the stock at the end of the day of purchase. You will find that country funds do not move as quickly as other stocks—there are not as many investors, so often the volume is low and the action is slow. Day trading country funds is not really possible. But with such great prospects for medium- to long-term investing, I am not sure why you would want to spend your entire day glued to a computer doing day trading anyway.

Short-term Trading/Investing

There really are no textbook definitions of trading periods. But if day trading is trading within a day, then short-term trading would be trading over periods longer than a day. Am I brilliant, or what? For country funds, I consider one week to one month to be short term, while one to a few days is day trading.

Short-term trading is desirable primarily during two situations:

1. When a stock drops dramatically in a short period of time, and you believe it will jump up quickly, the stock may not jump back up as quickly as you would like. You may be forced to hold on to it longer than a few days.

Sometimes our day and short-term trades end up being medium-term trades whether we like it or not. Unless the country or region is nearing record highs, I recommend being patient and waiting for the stock to move up again. The only time I sell and take a loss is when I need cash for more promising investments; when my analysis indicates that I can make more with the cash buying another stock than the loss from prematurely selling the other, I may sell at a loss.

2. When markets are slow and moving within support and resistance lines, you can buy a stock when its price hits the support line and sell a stock when its price hits its resistance. We discussed this in the last chapter. Instead of just sitting around waiting for a major drop, you can ride the waves, buying low and selling high. A number of 5 percent gains add up quickly to nice short-term profits. Some people can only dream of making 15 percent per year on their investments, when we can make 5 to 10 percent a month even in bear markets!

A note of caution: When a market has hit its peak and is on its way down, stay out of the market! You will know the market is overheated when everyone is getting rich and the market is setting records. If you buy at a high point, and the market starts its decline, the fall will happen quick and hard, and you will not have a chance to get out. What you thought was a short-term trade will turn into either a major loss or a five-year long-term "investment." Asian markets have still not returned to their 1994–1995 record heights! (By the way, during extremely active trading days, particularly during crashes, your online broker's web site and phone lines will be jammed, and most likely you will be unable to sell out.)

Medium- and Long-Term Investing

Determining when short-term trading becomes medium-term trading and when medium-term trading becomes long-term trading is difficult. The Internal Revenue Service (IRS) taxes *capital gains* from assets held more than one year at a lower rate than those sold within a year: 28 percent, compared to up to 38 percent.

Both medium- and long-term holdings would be considered investments, as opposed to day trading and short-term trading. With medium- and long-term country fund holdings, a person ideally is investing in countries he or she believes in.

> **capital gains** a tax assessed on profits realized from the sale of a capital asset, such as stock.

As I mentioned previously, my investments early in the next decade will be more long term, supplemented here and there by the other types. Every time we sell stock, the IRS takes away about one-third of our profits—and this is money we need to make us more money! (I picture every dollar in my portfolio as an employee working for me. The more employees I have, the more my company grows. If I fire employees, my production, and thus my profits, goes down. And I don't want that.)

RULE #7: Invest for the Long Term

Every major investment book I have ever read insists that the best way to maximize one's return in the long run is to invest long term. Studies have shown over and over again that people who turn over their portfolio frequently (i.e., day and short-term traders) do not make as much as those who stay put. Basically, it is too difficult to predict market peaks and valleys. Over time, it appears that stock markets gradually get higher and higher.

RULE #8: Buy Low, Sell High

Rules, like all things in life, have contradictions. One of the ways I made a tremendously high return (300 percent or so) in 1999 was from buying low and selling high. Because I had predicted that international markets would drop in late 1999 and throughout 2000, my goal was to liquidate my portfolio by summer's end. I wanted as much cash on hand in November and December when the markets took their big dive. So, throughout 1998 and 1999, I bought when markets hit their five-year lows, sold when they went up to their resistance levels, bought again when they fell, and so on—knowing the whole time (well, at least predicting) that I would never miss out by selling, because they would all fall again later in 2000 since U.S. markets were getting dangerously high.

The same buy low/sell high model can be used now, with slight modifications.

After you have carefully selected which funds you wish to invest in for the long term, eventually you will spend all of your investment cash. Is that it? Should you just sit back and wait a few years?

Possibly. *If* you want to have minimal risk.

But there are other ways to squeeze as much as possible from your "employees": Use leveraging.

"Tip" #9: Leveraging Can Make You Rich—or Poor

Leveraging is not a "rule"—I do not want to recommend this strategy to the fainthearted! Leveraging can make you rich; leveraging can also make you poor. I am offering it to you as a possible strategic tool.

As the word "leveraging" implies, you can leverage something to get more of something. In this case, money! There are two ways to leverage your investments, and both involve borrowing money.

One way is to borrow money from relatives. When I first started investing, after I became confident with my strategies, approaches, and intuition, I borrowed money from relatives, offering to pay them interest a few points above what they would get from treasury certificates and certificates of deposit. I also guaranteed their money: If I lost it, I would have to slave away in a real job for a few years to pay them back.

The other way to get more money is to take out a margin loan from your brokerage company. Most brokerage firms offer this service. Typically, firms will lend you $1 for every $1 you have in your account with them. Exceptions are stocks that they find high risk, such as technology and "penny stocks." Some companies will not provide loans for stock priced under a certain amount, such as $5 or $6; the U.S. Government restricts margin loans for stocks under $4^{1}/_{8}$. Typically, a company with a low-priced stock is not a strong company, or possibly it is just down on its luck. There is high probability that it may never recover or even may file for bankruptcy. However, country funds heading below $4 a share are not risky at all. Rather, this is the best time to buy them. But, unfortunately, we cannot take out margins loans during this time either, so loans from other sources may come in handy.

Leveraging is tricky, and there is definitely a particular strategy for using this very powerful tool.

Say that you have $50,000 to invest. Your brokerage company will provide you with a credit line of roughly another $50,000, so your total investment potential is $100,000. (As I mentioned, the credit line decreases if you invest in what the brokerage label "risky" stock (such as the Internet and technology).)

Begin by carefully buying up stock as country markets hit major lows. Eventually, these markets will go up, and so will the value of your portfolio. Leveraging makes a huge difference on your overall returns. For example, if you invested only $50,000 in five markets, and, on average, the markets go up 15 percent in a few months (which is not uncommon), you would make $7,500, which is not bad at all. However, if you fully extended your credit line and invested the full $100,000 in the same five stocks, you would have made $15,000. That's a 30 percent return on your initial investment.

Now, the broker extends your credit another $30,000! You can choose to "reinvest" this amount or have it go toward the $50,000 you borrowed. If you select this latter option, you now owe your broker only $20,000!

Once your initial portfolio base is built up, the trick is to buy additional stock only when a stock takes a major dive.

By the same token, you also can select to sell any of your holdings if they take a major jump up. You can sell the stock and buy it again later when it settles down again. There is always a risk, however, that the stock will keep climbing, and you will miss out on its longer-term potential. This is a call you will have to make, based on your research, intuition, and long-term strategy. And remember the tax considerations.

If you ever feel that you are overleveraged, if markets are getting too risky or overheated, or if you just want to take a slower approach, you always can sell off stock to cover the margin loan as your portfolio increases in value. That is actually my plan for the next few years: Take out as many loans as possible and buy as much stock as possible during the upcoming stock market crash; and as my portfolio rises, gradually pay back most of my loans, starting with the higher-interest loans. (I will most likely be leveraged around 300 percent at times!)

Oh, I forgot to mention that there is a slight cost to the money you will borrow. Brokers charge interest on all margin loans, and interest rates vary per broker. Chapter 6 explains which brokers charge the lowest rates. But, in general, interest runs around 9 percent on margin loans. This is not very much, considering the amount of money a person can make investing in emerging markets, however. Using the previous example, if you borrowed $50,000 for three months, you would owe approximately $875 in interest. But you made an extra $7,500. And interest is tax deductible.

Does this all sound too good to be true? Well, it may be. Stocks go down as easily as they go up. If your $100,000 dives the same amount, you will lose $15,000. It is a chance you will have to take. What you have on your side, however, is the fact that country funds, unlike companies, do not go out of business; unless an emerging market is reaching high levels or a major war or revolution breaks out in the country, eventually the stock will return to the level you purchased it at—you will just have to wait a bit.

And another warning here: When U.S. stock markets are volatile, brokers may, at their discretion, raise margin requirements. For example, my online broker, Firstrade.com, recently raised the price of stocks that it would margin from $4\frac{1}{8}$ to 5 and reduced the time to meet a *margin call* from nine business days to four business days. Now, as many of my stocks fluctuate around the $5 range, I only have four days to wire the broker money to cover my loan. Watch out for this.

> **margin call** a call from a broker to a customer (called a maintenance margin call) or from a clearinghouse to a clearing member (called a variation margin call) demanding the deposit of cash or marginable securities to satisfy U.S. government requirements and the house maintenance requirement for the purchase or short sale of securities or to cover an adverse price movement.

RULE #10: Don't Freak Out

Which brings me to my next point: Control yourself, damn it! You will find that you may become somewhat irrational, maybe even a crazed lunatic, when your portfolio drops 20 percent, and it appears that your life's savings are going down the drain. The financial news supports your fears because everyone else is freaking out too.

Markets go up, and they go down, like waves in the ocean. (I know, you are getting tired of me saying this, but even I often forget this concept under stressful situations.) When a stock market (or stock) sinks, market news is negative. When markets rise, everyone's excited, and the news is positive. You actually can feel the positive or negative energy if you closely follow the intraday charts and news. Fear spreads quite rapidly, convincing people to buy and sell when they normally would not.

Remember, unless the market you have invested in is hitting record highs, most likely it will go up again soon. Relax and stick to your original strategy. Emotions are an investor's worst enemy.

RULE #11: Don't Look Back

At first you may wish to check the prices of stock you sold to see if you would have made more or less if you sold at a different time, or how much you would have made if you purchased a stock at a particular time. Doing this is all very important for you to learn about how markets move and to develop a successful strategy for yourself.

Many people, however, continue to look back every time they sell a security. They are almost emotionally attached to the stock. This is a form of greed: "If I only waited one more day, I could have made another $1,000."

Maybe you could have made more money, but how would you have really known?

From my experience, I have found that a stock's chance of increasing the next day after a sale is the same as its chance for decreasing. It all evens out over time. What is important to me is that my overall buy and sell signals produce healthy profits. Whether I make a 3 percent return or a 25 percent return on a trade, it is better than most other investors are making. When people start to hold out for more and ignore their original plan, they are being greedy, and they definitely will lose in the long term.

Chapter 6

Online Brokers: Taking Control

IT'S SO EASY!

I can understand why many people get nervous about selecting an online broker: You are sending a large portion (or all) of your hard-earned savings to someone you don't know. I was nervous too, at first. When I started trading online, Internet trading was relatively new, and I knew few people who had accounts.

A friend recommended an online broker, Scottrade Securities. They had an office in my area, and the fees were the lowest around at the time—$7.95 for *market orders*. I went down to the office and met the staff, and gave them a check for $25,000—I wanted to try them out first before committing a more substantial amount of money.

market order a buy or sell order in which the broker is to execute the order at the best price currently available.

Today there are many respectable online brokers, most of which will not have a real office in your area. This really should not be a criterion for selecting one.

Many of the older, more established investment companies, such as Charles Schwab, have since entered the online brokerage game. So, if it is a real, physical office you want, there are brokers that offer them. Of course, you will have to pay for their comfy sofas and free coffee through higher transaction fees.

In the old days, most of us commoners, not as fortunate as the upper-class folk, would use an unconnected investment advisor from a major company such as Schwab or Smith Barney. We would meet with him or her every now and then—more then than now—to review our holdings and their plan for our money. There were few options. If we were not happy with our broker, we could change over to another. But honestly, they were all relatively the same.

And, oddly, for investment "experts," they did not seem to be *that* much better off than we were. I mean, if they were *so* financially savy, why weren't they driving a Rolls-Royce?

Overall, returns were average—the advisors were really just following the index as best they could. Costs were relatively high—3 percent or so of the value of our portfolio per year. (That's a big chunk! Possibly one-third of our yearly profits.)

But we were paying for *someone's* Rolls-Royce—Mr. Schwab's or Mr. Barney's. The boss was getting rich off of us, while we just barely kept up with inflation.

When the online brokers came along, offering us the opportunity to place our own trades for very low rates, all of the big companies started to get worried. Although this is America, some people love to try to control us. Especially if they are getting rich off of us. Fortunately, the Internet phenomenon grew so rapidly that they could not respond as quickly and effectively as they would have liked. If they had the time, I am sure they would have tried harder to try to regulate online brokers more, maybe charging them hefty fees, which would increase our overall costs of trading.

Lucky for us that this never happened. Now we no longer need the traditional investment advisors to "manage" our money; we can do it ourselves.

SELECTING A BROKER

An online broker is the same as an off-line broker, except that you can personally place your own orders to buy and sell securities over the Internet. Most online brokers have professional consultants you can speak with over the phone, if you require help getting started. Some even offer advisors you can meet with in person.

When I first started investing online, I probably called my broker a few times each day. This was all new to me, and I needed help. I had no idea what the difference between a market order and limit order was, let alone how to place either. It was a new world. The staff at my local Scottrade Securities office was quite useful.

Thus, contrary to what people might say, online brokers can be very helpful, even the ones that offer rock bottom prices.

I have read many broker comparison studies in respected financial sources. As a matter of fact, I would say that every major financial web site and publication has reviewed the subject at some point. Most of the surveys compare brokers along the following categories:

- ✔ *Costs:* commissions, minimum balances, minimum deposit required to open an account, margin rates, interest rates, and other fees
- ✔ *Quality:* responsiveness, statement clarity, broker knowledge, web site quality
- ✔ *Trading:* what types of instruments you can trade (i.e., stocks, mutual funds, bonds, treasuries, options, initial public offerings)
- ✔ *Services:* year-end statements, real-time quotes and research, touch-tone trading, check writing

Instead of boring you with the details of each of these categories, I will stick with information that is relevant for trading emerging market country funds: *Cost*. That's it. The rest is irrelevant.

"Are you crazy?" Maybe. But investing in emerging market funds does not require a sophisticated online brokerage service. Let's look at quality, trading, and services a little more to see why.

Quality refers to the quality of services a broker gives. Since most brokers do not have a clue about emerging markets, we really will not require their assistance for investment advice. We will need them for occasional help in learning about placing orders online and for placing an order over the phone. Almost all online brokers offer these services.

Another factor of quality is responsiveness and the quality of the web site. Obviously, we want a site that we can get into quickly and place an order. We don't want a site that is so busy that we cannot log on to it. Even the more expensive sites close down during busy periods. Every now and then, during the most active trading days, most sites either crash or are so busy that you cannot log on and place an order. So spending more on a broker is no guarantee of an effective and efficient online trading system.

The next factor listed to consider is *Trading*. Our country funds are simple stocks traded on NYSE and Nasdaq. All brokers offer this service, so it is not an issue when selecting a broker.

The final factor to consider is *Services*. I do admit that my monthly and yearly statements are a bit confusing. But, since I keep my own records, awkward account statements is not a major issue for me.

Some services may be important for you. As I mentioned previously, many online brokers offer free real-time stock quotes, stock quotes that automatically update in a window, and variations of this. However, I found the real issue is cost:

- ✔ How much does it cost to place a market order?
- ✔ How much does it cost to place a *limit order*?
- ✔ How much interest will you earn on uninvested cash?
- ✔ What is the interest rate for margin loans?

limit order an order to a broker to buy a specified quantity of a security at or below a specified price, or to sell it at or above a specified price (called the limit price).

These are the four issues that really matter. You can obtain research information from a zillion free sources these days. You need a basic, discount service that provides quick and reliable trades.

Let's look at a sample of online brokers to see how they stand up.

TAKING A CLOSER LOOK

Choosing the right online broker is important. If your investment plan is to start out small and make frequent transactions, obviously you will want low trading costs. For example, if you are trading $2,000 lots, looking for quick 3 to 5 percent turnovers, that would be a $60 to $100 gross profit. If you were using Schwab as your broker, at $29 per trade, your net gain would be decreased substantially. If, however, you used a discount broker, paying around $7 per trade, your net profits would not be affected as severely.

In my case, I plan to be highly leveraged at all times. I believe that I can make significantly more money using a margin loan than the interest I have to pay on the loan. And because I am dealing in larger sums of money, the actual transaction costs do not matter as much. What matters is the interest rate that I'm charged. One or two interest rate points can make a noticeable difference on yearly profits. For example, on a $100,000 loan, 1 to 2 percent is $1,000 to $2,000. You may think that is a small amount to squabble about, but I believe every dollar adds up.

On the other hand, you may not wish to be fully leveraged. You may even wish to have a good portion of your money in cash waiting for good buying opportunities. In this case, the amount of interest a broker pays on idle cash may be your deciding factor.

A list of online brokers follows. The list is not exhaustive. Rather, it is a selection of the top brokers, some large, others small, some expensive, others cheap. As you can see, most require no minimum deposit to open a cash account and $2,000 to open a margin account. (A cash account is a normal account without margin loan capabilities.) Once the broker receives your check and it clears, and you have completed an application, you are ready to start trading. You will be given a secret account number and will have to choose a password. If you wish to have a *margin account*, most likely you will have to complete another application. The broker wants to make sure you understand the risks of investing money that is not yours.

margin account a brokerage account in which the brokerage lends the customer cash with which to purchase securities.

Many brokers charge more for larger orders, usually orders for more than 5,000 shares. Most of our trades will be under 5,000 shares. Since most of our stocks trade between $5 and $10, you can buy between $25,000 to $50,000 or so without hitting the more than 5,000 share barrier. Keep in mind that the trade volume of our funds is not as high as blue chips' trade volume. Thus, we cannot trade big orders even if we wanted to. Unless you are planning to invest big money, I'm not sure this should be an issue.

When brokers offer margin loans, they may state their margin rates as a percentage greater or less than what they pay for the funds from their bank. The rate they pay is called the *broker call rate*, which is usually the same as the prime rate. The broker's rate recently was around 9 percent. The rates listed here are based on this 9 percent rate. The rate a broker charges customers usually decreases as the amount customers are borrowing increases.

For more information on online brokers, I highly recommend checking out Gomez.com's "Authoritative Guide to On-line Brokers." It lists the top brokers by overall score, ease of use, customer confidence, on-site resources, relationship services, and overall cost, and even suggests brokers by different investment styles.

> **broker call rate** interest rate that banks charge to brokers to finance margin loans to investors.

ONLINE BROKER REVIEW

Note: The first amount under minimum to open an account is the amount required to open a cash account; the second amount is that required to open a margin account. Many brokers pay interest on idle cash at the money market rate, which was around 5 percent at the time. Margin interest rates vary around the brokers' call rate and are stated as a percentage below or above this rate in the broker data that follows.

Ameritrade.com 800-454-9272

Minimum to Open:	$0—Cash/$2,000—Margin
Market Order:	$8
Limit Order:	$13
Interest Paid:	2.75 percent
Margin Interest:	<$25,000—0.75 percent above brokers' call
	$25,000–50,000—+0.25 percent above brokers' call
Streaming Data:	No

BrownCo.com 800-225-6707

Minimum to Open:	$15,000
Market Order:	$5 ($.01/share > 5,000 shares)
Limit Order:	$10 ($.01/share>5,000 shares)

Interest Paid:	2.75 percent
Margin Interest:	<$50,000—brokers' call
	>$1 million—varies
Streaming Data:	No

Datek.com 800-U2-Datek

Minimum to Open:	$0/$2,000
Market Order:	$9.99
Limit Order:	$9.99
Interest Paid:	4.25 percent
Margin Interest:	<$50,000—+0.5
	>$50,000—brokers' call
Streaming Data:	Yes

DLJDirect.com 800-825-5723

Minimum to Open:	None
Market Order:	$20.00 (>1,000, $.02/share)
Limit Order:	$20.00 (>1,000, $.02/share)
Interest Paid:	3.5 percent
Margin Interest:	<$25,000—+1.5%
	>$25,000—varies
Streaming Data:	Yes ($25/month)

ETrade.com 800-ETRADE1

Minimum to Open:	$1,000/$2,000
Market Order:	$14.95 (>5,000, $.01/Share)
Limit Order:	$19.95 (>5,000, $.01/Share)
Interest Paid:	Money market
Margin Interest:	<$25,000—+0.25%
	>$25,000—varies
Streaming Data:	Yes ($35/month)

Fidelity.com 800-544-6666

Minimum to Open:	\$5,000
Market Order:	\$14.95 (>1,000, \$.02/share)
Limit Order:	\$19.95 (>1,000, \$.02/share)
Interest Paid:	4.49 percent
Margin Interest:	<\$10,000—+2%
	>\$10,000—varies
Streaming Data:	Yes

FirstTrade.com 888-998-6168

to Open:	\$0/\$2,000
Market Order:	\$6.95
Limit Order:	\$9.95
Interest Paid:	4.25 percent
Margin Interest:	<\$100,000——½ percent
	>\$100,000—¾ percent
Streaming Data:	Yes

Morgan Stanley (www.online.msdw.com) 800-688-6896

Minimum to Open:	\$2,000
Market Order:	\$29.95 (>1,000, \$.03/share)
Limit Order:	\$29.95 (>1,000, \$.03/share)
Interest Paid:	Money market (around 5 percent now)
Margin Interest:	<\$5,000—+2.5 percent
	>\$5,000—varies
Streaming Data:	No

MyDiscountBroker.com 888-882-5600

Minimum to Open:	\$0/\$2,000
Market Order:	\$12 (>5,000, \$.01/share)
Limit Order:	\$12 (>5,000, \$.01/share)

Interest Paid:	Money market
Margin Interest:	+0.75 percent
Streaming Data:	No

NDB.com 888-302-7764

Minimum to Open:	None
Market Order:	$14.75 (>5,000, $.001/share)
Limit Order:	$19.75 (>5,000, $.001/share)
Interest Paid:	Money market
Margin Interest:	<$10,000—+1 percent
	>$10,000–$25,000—0.5 percent
Streaming Data:	No

ScotTrade.com 800-619-SAVE

Minimum to Open:	$500/$2,000
Market Order:	$7
Limit Order:	$12
Interest Paid:	4.25 percent
Margin Interest:	–0.75%
Streaming Data:	No

SureTrade.com 401-642-6900

Minimum to Open:	$0/$2,000
Market Order:	$7.95
Limit Order:	$9.95
Interest Paid:	Money market
Margin Interest:	<$50,000—–0.5 percent
	>$50,000—varies
Streaming Data:	No

TradingDirect.com 212-766-0241

Minimum to Open:	\$0/\$2,000
Market Order:	\$9.95
Limit Order:	\$9.95
Interest Paid:	Brokers' call less 3 percent
Margin Interest:	<\$100,000—–0.5 percent
	>\$100,000—varies

Note: Out of all of the brokers I called, Trading Direct was the only one that had a terribly rude and obnoxious phone representative . . . twice!

Streaming Data:	No

Waterhouse.com 800-934-4410

Minimum to Open:	\$1,000/\$2,000
Market Order:	\$12 (>5,000, \$.01/share)
Limit Order:	\$12 (>5,000, \$.01/share)
Interest Paid:	Money market
Margin Interest:	<\$50,000—+1 percent
	>\$50,000—+½ percent
Streaming Data:	No

WebStreet.com 800-WEB-TRADE

Minimum to Open:	\$0/\$2,000
Market Order:	\$14.95
Limit Order:	\$14.95
Interest Paid:	Money Market
Margin Interest:	<\$5,000—+2 percent
	>\$25,000—+0.75 percent

Note: Nasdaq stock trades of 1,000 shares or more, and priced over \$2, are *free*! (Most of our country funds, however, trade on NYSE.)

Streaming Data:	No

I can't advise you which broker you should use. I suppose they all have their strengths and weaknesses (although I cannot see why anyone would want to pay more than $10 for a market order; the expensive sites also seem to have weaker margin and interest deals).

I've used Scottrade for the last few years and had good luck with them. It was somewhat comforting to know that they had a physical office nearby. Actually, when you call their 800 number, your call gets directed to their local office. They are like a good neighbor!

However, I recently moved some of my money to First Trade because of their low margin rates and low trading fees. I suggest you visit each broker's web site and see which you feel most comfortable with.

BUYING AND SELLING

Buying and selling stock over the Internet is really quite easy. At first I was nervous—imagine that, at the click of a button, I could send an order out to purchase stock. Once I gave the final click, there was no turning back. I also had a lot of questions about how to read stock quotes and the difference between the various types of orders (i.e., market, limit, options, etc.)

Most online brokers have key information separated into the following three main categories, among others:

1. Market data
2. Trading
3. Portfolio information

Market Data

Market data include stock quotes, research, and other general information. Many brokers have alliances with financial news sites and research organizations and provide limited or unlimited access to these sites. Users can research companies and call up charts. I have never accessed this type of market information from my broker's site. Country fund investments require information that is not available from most research sources. Furthermore, most of this information can be gathered from popular financial sites for free (Yahoo!, Amazon, etc.)

If you do not plan to purchase Window on Wall Street's software or a comparable product and use a real-time data service, brokers offer customers real-time stock quotes for free. The only problem is that with your broker's free service, you may have to sit there at your computer and continue to click to get updated prices, which can be a pain.

A stock quote consists of the following standard information:

Symbol the stock's symbol (IF for Indonesia Fund, etc.).
Last the price of the last trade in the market.
Change either percent or stock price change from the previous day's closing price.
Size the number of shares traded during the "last" trade.
Bid the current market price being offered for a security.
Ask this is the current market price you will have to pay for a security.
Size the number of shares currently at the bid and ask price. If the size was "24x20" there would be 2,400 shares up for sale at the bid price and 2,000 shares reading to buy at the ask price.
High the day's highest price.
Low the day's lowest price.
Volume the number of shares of the stock treated during the day.
Market which market the stock is traded on (NYSE, Nasdaq, etc.)

Understanding how to read the "size" is the only real tricky part. Just remember to add two zeros on the end, and you should be fine.

Trading

Each broker's web site has a special place to buy and sell stocks. Each broker requires seven areas of information to place an order:

1. *Transaction Type:* Buy, sell, sell short, and buy-to-cover short. We need to be concerned only with buy and sell for country funds. If you want to buy a stock, select "Buy"; if you want to sell a stock, select "Sell."
2. *Quantity:* The number of shares you wish to buy or sell. (Remember to double check the quantity a few times before your final click.)
3. *Symbol:* The symbol of the stock you wish to buy or sell (IF, etc.). (Make sure to double check this a few times too.)
4. *Order Type:* There are four basic order types:
   a. *Market Order:* The order is executed immediately as soon as it hits the trading floor at the best available price.

      Note that larger orders may be broken up into smaller orders depending on supply and demand for the stock. For example, if you place a market order to sell 5,000 shares of a stock, there might be a need for only 1,000 shares at the current ask price. The remaining 4,000 shares will be sold at the new ask price, which could be higher or lower than what you had hoped. Larger orders may take longer to execute completely.

      Note that your broker charges you for each split, so you may end up paying for two or more orders.

      From my experience, market orders usually are not split more than once, and I have received a better price on the second order just as often as I have received a worse price.
   b. *Limit Order:* This is an order for which you set a maximum price that you are willing to pay for a stock or a minimum price you are willing to accept as a seller.

      Limit orders have a number of very powerful uses. First, you can keep your order from being broken up, as discussed above. Second, and one of the most useful benefits, is that you can conduct your research in the evening and set limit orders for stocks you want to buy or sell for the next day. Then you don't have to baby-sit your computer the whole day as your orders will be executed automatically if your desired price is reached.

The bad news is that a stock's price may not reach your set limit and thus your order will never be placed. I have also watched the market price hit my limit price and *not* execute. The most likely reasons were that my order size was too large, there were other orders ahead of me, or market conditions changed.

If you really want to buy or sell something, the only guaranteed way of doing so is through a market order. You just might not get the price you want.

c. *Stop Order:* I have never used a stop order. A *stop order* becomes activated and turns into a market order once the stock trades at or through the stop price specified by you. Once your stock hits a certain price, the order becomes activated. You are guaranteed an execution, but not at any particular price.

stop order a market order to buy or sell a certain quantity of a certain security if a specified price (the stop price) is reached or passed.

A limit order can be executed only at a certain price; if your order is executed, it will do so at the price you specify. A stop order is similar, except you are not guaranteed a certain price. It is, in effect, a market order set to go off at a certain price.

Some people use stop orders to limit the amount they can lose in market crashes. As you know, markets can crash at any time, without notice, especially during turbulent markets conditions and when entering a bear market. You can set stop orders to set your stocks free in situations like this. The only problem with this strategy is that stocks often fluctuate quite a bit during the day and may drop down for just a short period of time, setting off your stop order and selling your stock prematurely.

d. *Stop Limit Order:* This is similar to a stop order in that it becomes activated once it reaches your set price. However, once activated, the stop limit order becomes a limit order and can be executed only at the set limit price or better. Thus, an execution is not guaranteed.

I have not yet found a use for stop limit orders with country funds.

5. *Limit or Stop Price:* If your order is not a market order, but rather a limit or stop order, you need to enter the price at which you wish to buy or sell the security.

6. *Duration*

   ✔ *Day Order:* The order stays open for only the current trading day; the order will be canceled when the markets close at the end of the day.

   ✔ *GTC:* "Good till canceled" orders stay open until the order is executed or you cancel your order.

7. *Qualifiers:* Other instructions on your order. Not all brokers offer the entire selection listed below.

   ✔ *None:* Select "none" if you do not want any further qualifier attached to your order.

   ✔ *AON:* AON orders are qualified as "all or none." A buy or sell order can be marked AON to signify that no partial transaction is to be executed. Most brokers limit this qualifier to limit orders. I like this qualifier because it keeps my order from being broken up.

   ✔ *DNR:* DNR orders are qualified as "do not reduce." A limit order to buy, a stop order to sell, or a stop-limit order to sell can be marked so that it is never reduced. This is similar to all or none.

- ✔ *AON DNR:* AON DNR orders are qualified as both all or none and do not reduce. An order can be marked AON DNR to signify that no partial transaction is to be executed and it is not to be reduced. If a broker offers this option, it may be limited to limit orders.
- ✔ *OPG:* OPG orders are qualified as "at the opening." An OPG qualifier requires your order to be executed at the opening price. If not executed at the opening, it will be canceled. If a broker offers this option, it may be limited to market orders.
- ✔ *CLO:* CLO orders are qualified as "at the close." A CLO qualifier requests that your order be executed as close to the closing price as possible. There is no guarantee that the price will be the closing price.
- ✔ *FOK:* FOK orders are qualified as "fill or kill." A FOK qualifier requires the immediate purchase or sale of your entire specified quantity of stock, although not necessarily at one price. If the entire order cannot be filled immediately, it is automatically canceled (killed). This qualifier often cannot be used on market orders.
- ✔ *IOC:* IOC orders are qualified as "immediate or cancel." An IOC qualifier requires the immediate execution of all or part of your specified quantity of stock. Any portion of the order not executed immediately is canceled. This qualifier often cannot be used for over-the-counter (OTC) stocks and cannot be used on market orders.

THAT'S ALL, FOLKS!

That is all there is to it. You now have all of the information you need to plan an investment strategy and build a strong portfolio. If you need assistance when first placing an order, please do not hesitate to call your broker. Although brokers prefer that you conduct your trading online, they can be of great help when learning the ropes.

And don't worry about getting on their nerves—you are just one of hundreds or thousands of people calling them each day. They probably won't recognize your voice! This is your hard-earned cash, so take your time until you get the information you are after and you feel comfortable buying and selling.

Good luck, and have fun!

Glossary

analysis the examination and evaluation of relevant information to select the best course of action from among various alternatives.

ask the lowest price that any investor or dealer has declared that he or she will sell a given security or commodity for. For over-the-counter stocks, the ask is the best quoted price at which a market maker is willing to sell a stock. For mutual funds, the ask is the net asset value plus any sales charges. Also called asked price, asking price, or offering price.

bear market a prolonged period of falling prices, usually by 20 percent or more, accompanied by widespread pessimism.

beta a quantitative measure of the volatility of a given stock, mutual fund, or portfolio, relative to the overall market, usually the Standard & Poor's (S&P) 500. Specifically, the performance the stock, fund, or portfolio has experienced in the last five years as the S&P moved 1 percent up or down. A beta above 1 is more volatile than the overall market, while a beta below 1 is less volatile.

bid the highest price any buyer is willing to pay for a given security at a given time; also called bid price.

blue chip stock of a large, national company with a solid record of stable earnings and/or dividend growth and a reputation for high-quality management and/or products. More generally, anything of very high quality.

bond a debt instrument issued for a period of more than one year with the purpose of raising capital by borrowing. The federal government, states, cities, corporations, and many other types of institutions sell bonds. A bond is generally a promise to repay the principal along with interest on a specified date (maturity).

broker an individual or firm that acts as an intermediary between a buyer and seller, usually charging a commission. To sell securities and most other products, a license is required.

broker call rate interest rate that banks charge to brokers to finance margin loans to investors.

bull market a prolonged period of rising prices, usually by 20 percent or more.

capital cash or goods used to generate income.

capital gains a tax assessed on profits realized from the sale of a capital asset, such as stock.

chart a graph of the price movements of a given security over a given time period, sometimes along with volume data. (*See* **volume**.)

charter a document, filed with a U.S. state by a corporation's founders, describing the purpose, place of business, and other details of a corporation.

close the price of the last transaction for a given security at the end of a given trading session.

closed-end fund a fund with a fixed number of shares outstanding, and one that does not redeem shares the way a typical mutual fund does. Such funds often are listed on a major stock exchange and trade like other securities. Unlike a typical mutual fund, a closed-end fund's share price can trade above or below its net asset value.

cyclical something that happens periodically, that is, on a regular basis.

day trade the purchase and sale of the same security on the same day.

delayed not current, as with quotes or news.

diversification a portfolio strategy designed to reduce exposure to risk by combining a variety of investments, such as stocks, bonds, and real estate, that are unlikely to move in the same direction at the same time.

diversified portfolio a collection of investments all owned by the same individual or organization containing a variety of investments that are unlikely to move in the same direction.

dividend a taxable payment declared by a company's board of directors and given to its shareholders out of the company's current or retained earnings, usually quarterly. Usually it is given as cash (cash dividend), but it also can take the form of stock (stock dividend) or other property. Also called payout.

earnings per share (EPS) total earnings divided by the number of shares outstanding. Companies often use a weighted average of outstanding stock over the reporting term.

emerging market a financial market of a developing country, usually a small market with a short operating history.

fund manager the individual responsible for making portfolio decisions for a mutual fund, pension fund, or insurance fund.

fundamental analysis a method of security valuation that involves examining the company's financials and operations, especially sales, earnings, growth potential, assets, debt, management, products, and competition.

fundamentals the basics, as of a business.

historical data past information about a company, used to help forecast the company's future; for example, historical price, price/earnings ratio, revenues and revenue growth, earnings and earnings growth.

index fund a passively managed mutual fund that tries to mirror the performance of a specific index, such as the Standard & Poor's 500. Since portfolio decisions are automatic and transactions are infrequent, expenses tend to be lower than those of actively managed funds.

indicator data that provide information about or predict the overall health of the economy or the financial markets; examples are inflation, interest rates, employment, and volume.

inflation the overall general upward price movement of goods and services in an economy, usually as measured by the Consumer Price Index and the Producer Price Index.

interest rates interest per year divided by principal amount, expressed as a percentage.

investing using money to make more money, usually with the understanding that risk is something to be avoided unless adequately compensated for. Often done by purchasing items of value for income or capital appreciation, such as stocks, bonds, mutual funds, unit investment trusts, real estate, money market funds, and collectibles.

investment an item of value purchased for income or capital appreciation.

leverage the degree to which an investor or business is utilizing borrowed money.

liability a financial obligation, debt, claim, or potential loss.

limit order an order to a broker to buy a specified quantity of a security at or below a specified price, or to sell it at or above a specified price (called the limit price).

margin account a brokerage account in which the brokerage lends the customer cash with which to purchase securities.

margin call a call from a broker to a customer (called a maintenance margin call) or from a clearinghouse to a clearing member (called a variation margin call) demanding the deposit of cash or marginable securities to satisfy U.S. government requirements and the house maintenance requirement for the purchase or short sale of securities or to cover an adverse price movement.

margin loan a loan to purchase securities provided by a broker to clients.

market order a buy or sell order in which the broker is to execute the order at the best price currently available.

moving average a technical analysis term meaning the average price of a security over a specified time period. Used in order to spot pricing trends by flattening out large fluctuations.

mutual fund an open-ended fund operated by an investment company that raises money from shareholders and invests in a group of assets, in accordance with a stated set of objectives. Benefits include diversification and professional money management. Shares are issued and redeemed on demand, based on the fund's net asset value, which is determined at the end of each trading session. A closed-end fund often is incorrectly referred to as a mutual fund; actually it is an investment trust.

open the first price of a given security or commodity in a trading session.

open-end fund the same as a mutual fund. A closed-end fund often is incorrectly referred to as a mutual fund; but actually it is an investment trust.

order a request from a client to a broker to buy (buy order) or sell (sell order) a specified amount of a particular security or commodity at a specific price or at the market price.

portfolio a collection of investments all owned by the same individual or organization.

price/earnings (P/E) ratio the most common measure of how expensive a stock is; equal to a stock's capitalization divided by its after-tax earnings over a 12-month period.

quote the highest bid or lowest ask price available on a security at any given time.

real time current, as with quotes or news; opposite of delayed.

recession a period of general economic decline; specifically, a decline in gross domestic product for two or more consecutive quarters.

resistance inability of a stock to rise above a certain price (its resistance level).

risk the quantifiable likelihood of loss or less-than-expected returns.

security an investment instrument, other than an insurance policy or fixed annuity, issued by a corporation, government, or other organization that offers evidence of debt or equity.

Securities and Exchange Commission (SEC) the primary federal regulatory agency for the securities industry, whose responsibility it is to promote full disclosure and to protect investors against fraudulent and manipulative practices in the securities markets.

share certificate representing one unit of ownership in a corporation, mutual fund, or limited partnership.

stock an instrument that signifies an ownership position, or equity, in a corporation and represents a claim on its proportionate share in the corporation's assets and profits.

stock exchange an exchange on which shares of stock and common stock equivalents are bought and sold.

stop order a market order to buy or sell a certain quantity of a certain security if a specified price (the stop price) is reached or passed.

support in technical analysis, a price level that a security has had difficulty falling below.

symbol a system of letters used to identify uniquely a stock or mutual fund.

technical analysis a method of evaluating securities by relying on the assumption that market data, such as charts of price, volume, and open interest, can help predict future (usually short-term) market trends. Unlike fundamental analysis, the technical analysis does not consider intrinsic value of the security.

trend the current general direction of movement for prices or rates.

trendline technical analysis formation created by drawing a line connecting a series of descending tops, descending bottoms, ascending tops, or ascending bottoms.

U.S. Fed the seven-member Board of Governors that oversees Federal Reserve Banks, establishes monetary policy (interest rates, credit, etc.), and monitors the economic health of the United States.

volatility the relative rate at which the price of a security moves up and down; found by calculating the annualized standard deviation of daily change in price.

volume the number of shares, bonds, or contracts traded during a given period, for a security or an entire exchange.

Index

Active trading, 163
African market, South Africa, 96–98
Alliance Capital Management, 98, 109
Amazon.com, 8, 123, 185
American Stock Exchange (AMEX), 115, 119–120
American stock exchanges, 19
American Stock Transfer and Trust Company, 58, 98, 105
America Online (AOL), 8, 124, 140
Ameritrade.com, 179
Analysis, defined, 13. *See* Fundamental analysis; Stock analysis; Technical analysis
Andrew's pitchfork, 141
AON (all or none) orders, 188
AON DNR orders, 189
Arcs, 140-141
Argentina:
  country brief, 77–79
  index fund, 79–80, 132
Argentina Fund, Inc., The (AF), 79–80, 132
Asian flu, 66
Asian markets:
  Australia, 27–29
  China, 30-32
  Hong Kong, 33–36
  India, 37–40
  Indonesia, 41–44
  Japan, 45–48
  Korea, 49–52
  Malaysia, 53–55
  Pakistan, 56–58
  Philippines, 59–61
  Singapore, 62–64
  Taiwan, 65–67
  Thailand, 68–71
  Vietnam, 72–75
Asian stock market, 13–14
Ask, 23, 120
Australia:
  country brief, 27–28
  index funds, 28–29

Barron's Guide to Making Investment Decisions (Prestbo/Sease), 113
Bear markets, 147, 187
Beta, 151–152
Bid, 23, 120
BigCharts.com, 115, 124, 129
Blue chips, 15, 20, 178
Board of Governors, 14
Bonds, 6–7, 67
Book of International Investing: Everything You Need to Know About Investing in Foreign Markets (Prestbo/Sease), 113
Boston Equiserve, 55, 71
Brazil:
  country brief, 81–83
  index funds, 84
Brazil Fund, Inc., The (BZF), 84, 152
Brazilian Equity Fund, Inc. (BZL), 84
Broker(s):
  defined, 13
  online, *see* Online brokers
  selection factors, 175–177

Brokerage firms, services provided by, 168. *See also* Online brokers
Broker call rate, 178–179
BrownCo.com, 179–180
Bull markets, 6–7, 147
Bureau of Labor Statistics, 24
Bureau of the Census, 24
Buy low, sell high strategy, 7–16, 167
Buy signal, 140, 147–148

Capital, 20
Capital gains, 166
Catastrophic events, impact of, 24, 136, 163–164
Central Intelligence Agency, 24
Channel trendline, 138
Chart(s), *see* Charting; *specific types of trendlines*
  analysis, 154
  defined, 121
  information resources, 115, 124, 129
Charter, 20
Charting, investment software, 121–124
Chile:
  country brief, 85–87
  index fund, 87–88
Chile Fund, Inc., The (CH), 87–88
China:
  country brief, 30–32
  fundamentals of, 24
  index funds, 32, 34–36
China Fund, Inc., The (CHN), 9–10, 20, 34
CLO (at the close) orders, 189
Close, 133–134
Closed-end funds:
  characteristics of, generally, 19–20, 23
  country funds, 8, 137
  defined, 4–5
  open-end funds compared with, 21–23
  single-country, 129
CNNfn, 124, 158
Commodity Channel Index, 145–148
Country funds, overview:
  Africa, 92, 96–98
  Argentina, 77–80
  Asian markets, 26–75
  Australia, 27–29
  Brazil, 81–84
  Chile, 85–88
  China, 24, 30–32
  "developing" European markets, 99–109
  fundamentals, generally, 23–24, 153–154
  Hong Kong, 33–36
  India, 37–40
  Indonesia, 41–44
  Israel, 93–95
  Japan, 45–48
  Korea, 49–52
  Malaysia, 53–55
  Mexico, 89–91
  Middle East market, 92–95
  Pakistan, 56–58
  Philippines, 59–61
  Portugal, 100–102
  Russia, 24, 103–106
  Singapore, 62–64
  South Africa, 96–98
  South American markets, 76–91
  Spain, 107–109
  Taiwan, 65–67
  Thailand, 68–71
  Turkey, 24, 110–112
  Vietnam, 72–75
Credit Suisse Asset Management, 44, 88, 95, 102
Cumulative dividend equity, 153
Current dividend yield, 153
Cycle lines, 141

Daiwa Securities Trust Company, 48, 64, 67, 70
Data collection, forms of, 118
Datek.com, 180
Day orders, 188

Day trader software, 127
Day traders:
  characteristics of, 163
  software for, 127
  trades, types of, *see* Day trading
Day trading, 114, 156, 162–164
Delayed data, 118
Delayed quotes, 12
Developing country funds, 5
Disney, 121–122
Diversification, *see* Diversified portfolio
  country, 162
  importance of, 5–7, 162
  regional, 162
Diversified portfolio:
  benefits of, 5
  defined, 6
  suggestions for, 6
Dividends, 115–116, 153
DLJDirect.com, 180
DNR (do not reduce) orders, 188–189
Dow Jones Industrial Average, 9, 14, 21, 136, 151–152

Earnings per share (EPS), 115–116, 120, 153
Emerging market, defined, 2
Emotions, control of, 157, 161, 170–171
End of day data, 118
ETrade.com, 180
European markets, "developing":
  Portugal, 100–102
  Russia, 103–106
  Spain, 107–109
  Turkey, 110–112
European Monetary Union (EMU), 101
Exponential moving average, 143–144

Fans, 140–141
Federal Reserve, 14
Fees:
  investment advisor, 12
  online brokers, 173, 176
  open-end mutual funds, 22
Fibonacci arcs, 141
Fibonacci fans, 141
Fibonacci time zones, 141
Fidelity.com, 181
Financial advisors:
  fees, 12
  role of, 5–6, 11–12, 14, 16, 174
  trust and, 20
Financial data, investment software, 128–129
Financial ratios, 136
First Australia Fund (IAF), 23, 28–29
First Israel Fund (ISL), 95
First Philippine Fund, Inc., The (FPF), 60–61
FirstTrade.com, 170, 181, 184
FOK (fill or kill) orders, 189
Fund management team, role of, 20
Fund managers, role of, 14–15
Fundamental analysis, 136–137
Fundamentals, 24

Gann angles, 141
Gann retracement, 141
Generic indicators:
  arcs, 140–141
  fans, 140–141
  trendlines, 137–140
Getting started, 155–160
Gomez.com, 178
Greater China Fund, Inc., The (GCH), 35
Greed, 171
Gross domestic product, 7. *See also specific countries*
GTC (good till canceled) orders, 188

Historical data, 115–116, 118, 157–159
Hong Kong:
  country brief, 33–34
  index funds, 34–36
Hong Kong Hang Seng Index, 9, 21, 117
Hong Kong Stock Exchange, 20

Hong Kong WEBS Index Series (EWH), 35
Hot stock tips, 13

IBM, 15, 19
Index fund, 14–15, 21
India:
  country brief, 37–38
  index funds, 38–40
India Fund, Inc., The (IFN), 38–39
Indicators:
  defined, 125
  fundamental, 152–154
  generic, 137–141
  technical, 141–152
Indonesia:
  country brief, 41–43
  index fund, 43–44
Indonesia Fund, Inc., The (IF), 16–18, 43–44
Inflation, 8–9, 136. *See also specific countries*
Information resources:
  Barron's Guide to Making Investment Decisions (Prestbo/Sease), 113
  Book of International Investing: Everything You Need to Know About Investing in Foreign Markets (Prestbo/Sease), 113
  on investment software, 128–129
  on online brokers, 178–179
  www.Washingtonpost.com, 126, 158
Interest rates, 8, 14, 18, 136
Internal Revenue Service (IRS), 166
International financial instruments, suggested portfolios, 6
International Monetary Fund (IMF), 42, 69, 82
Internet:
  as information resource, 4, 12, 126, 158
  online investment services, 12. *See also* Online brokers
Internet stocks, 168
Intraday chart, 122–123
Intrinsic value, 135
Inventor psychology, 140
Investing, defined, 114
Investment, defined, 2
Investment horizon, 161
Investment philosophy, 147
Investment potential:
  country funds, 24
  in emerging markets, generally, 16–18
Investment software:
  categories of, 118
  day trader, 127
  financial data options, 128–129
  nonprofessional tools, 119–165
  professional tools, 126–128
  purposes of, 118
  sources of, 115
  Window on Wall Street Internet Trader Pro 7.0, 115, 120, 125, 127–128
Investment strategies, *see* Buy low, sell high strategy
  basic time strategies, 161–171
  getting started, 155–161
  historical data, analysis of, 157–160
  leveraging, 167–169
  time frame models, 156
Investment trusts, *see* Open-end funds
Investors Bank and Trust Company, 112
IOC (immediate or cancel) orders, 189
Israel:
  country brief, 93–94
  index fund, 95

Jakarta Stock Exchange, 16
Japan:
  country brief, 45–47
  index funds, 47–48
Japan Equity Fund, Inc., The (JEQ), 48
Japan WEBS Index Series (EWJ), 47

Jardine Fleming India Fund, Inc. (JFI), 39–40

Korea:
- country brief, 49–51
- index funds, 51–52

Korea Equity Fund, Inc. (KEF), 51
Korea Fund, Inc., The (KF), 52

Latin America, open-end funds, 1
Level 2 data, 118–119
Leverage, 4–5, 18, 156, 167, 177
Liability, 137
Limit orders, 176–177, 186–187
Limit price, 188
Long-term investing strategies, 156, 166–171
Long-term investment potential, 24

MACD (moving average convergence divergence), 148–150
Maintenance margin call, 170
Malaysia:
- country brief, 53–54
- index funds, 54–55

Malaysia Fund, Inc., The (MF), 55
Malaysia WEBS Index Series (EWM), 54–55
Margin account, 178
Margin call, 170
Margin loans:
- applications of, 17, 168–169
- defined, 4–5
- interest on, 169
- overleveraged, 169
- sources of, 178

Market corrections, 14
Market order, 173, 186
Market trends, 135
Maturity, 7
Media, influence of, 159
Medium-term investing strategies, 156, 166
Medium-term investment potential, 24
Mercosur, 86
Mexico:
- country brief, 89–90
- index funds, 91

Mexico Fund, Inc., The (MXF), 91, 143, 145–146
Mexico WEBS Index Series (EWW), 91
Microsoft (MSFT), 15, 127
Microsoft Excel, 126
Middle East market, Israel, 93–95
Mitchell Hutchins Asset Management, 35, 40
Mobil, 15, 19
Money flow index, 122, 150–151
Morgan Stanley (www.online.msdw.com), 181
Morgan Stanley Dean Witter Africa Investment Fund, Inc. (AFF), 97–98
Morgan Stanley funds:
- Morgan Stanley Dean Witter Africa Investment Fund, Inc. (AFF), 97–98
- Morgan Stanley India Investment Fund, Inc. (IIF), 39
- Morgan Stanley Russia and New Europe Fund, Inc. (RNE), 105

Morgan Stanley India Investment Fund, Inc. (IIF), 39
Morgan Stanley Russia and New Europe Fund, Inc. (RNE), 105
Moving average, 141–144
Mutual funds:
- capital, 20
- charter, 20
- defined, 4, 20

MyDiscountBroker.com, 181–182

Nasdaq (National Association of Securities Dealers), 10, 19, 115, 120, 176, 183
Nasdaq Composite Index, 10–11
Nasdaq Level 2 window, 127–128
NDB.com, 182

Nonprofessional tools, stock analysis software:
  portfolio manager, 126
  powerful charting, 121–124
  streaming data, 119–121
  technical analysis, 124–125
North American Free Trade Agreement (NAFTA), 90
NYSE (New York Stock Exchange), 19–20, 115, 119, 176, 183

Online brokers:
  buying and selling transactions, 184–189
  fees, 173, 176
  information resources, 178–179
  interest paid, 177
  market data, 184–185
  opening an account, 178–179
  order placement, 186–189
  quality of service, 176
  review of, 179–184
  selection factors, 173–177
  services provided by, 4, 118, 120–121, 124, 126, 161
  stock market quotes, components of, 185
Online investment services:
  function of, 12
  trust in, 13
Open, 133
Open-end funds:
  closed-end funds distinguished from, 21–23
  defined, 1
  drawbacks to, 22
OPG (at the opening) orders, 189
Orders, 11–12, 160–161, 186–189. *See also specific types of orders*
Organization for Economic Cooperation and Development (OECD), 28, 111
Oscillators, 141
Overleveraged, 169

Pakistan:
  country brief, 56–57
  index fund, 58
Pakistan Investment Fund, Inc. (PKF), 58
Penny stocks, 168
Philippines:
  country brief, 59–60
  index fund, 60–61
Portfolio:
  control over, 13–16
  defined, 22
  diversification, *see* Diversification; Diversified portfolio
Portfolio manager, investment software, 126
Portugal:
  country brief, 100–101
  index fund, 102
Portugal Fund, Inc., The (PGF), 102
Prestbo, John, 113
Price chart, 123
Price/earnings (P/E) ratio, 153–154
Price oscillator, 144–145
Professional tools, stock analysis software, 125–128

Quadrant lines, 141
Quotes, 12

Range, 132
Real estate investments, 6
Real time data, 118
Real time quotes, 12
Recession
  in Argentina, 78
  Asian market, 8, 11, 17
  defined, 6–7
  emerging from, 17–18
Relative strength index, 10
Resistance, 138–139, 167
Resistance trendlines, 138–140, 158
Reuter's, 3
Risk, 11, 18, 156, 169

Russia:
country brief, 103–105
fundamentals of, 24
index funds, 105–106

Schwab, 174
ScotTrade.com, 182, 184
Scottrade Securities, 173, 175, 184
Scudder Stevens & Clark, Inc., 52, 80
Sease, Doug, 113
Securities and Exchange Commission (SEC), 136–137
Sell signal, 140, 147–148
Shanghai Stock Exchange, 20
Share, defined, 22
Shenzen Stock Exchange, 20
Short-term investment potential, 24
Short-term trading/investing strategies, 156, 165–166
Simple moving average, 143
Singapore:
country brief, 62–63
index funds, 63–64
Singapore Fund, Inc., The:
Singapore (SGF), 64
Taiwan (TYW), 67
Singapore WEBS Index Series (EWS), 63–64
Single-country funds, 114–115
Smith Barney, 174
South Africa:
country brief, 96–97
index funds, 97–98
South American markets:
Argentina, 77–80
Brazil, 81–84
Chile, 85–88
Mexico, 25, 89–91
Southern Africa Fund, Inc., The (SOA), 98
Spain:
country brief, 107–108
index funds, 108–109
Spain Fund, Inc., The (SNF), 109
Spain WEBS Index Series (EWP), 108
Standard & Poor's 500, 15, 151
Standard Chartered Bank, 3, 21
Standard deviation, 8
State Street Bank & Trust, 34
Stock analysis, basics of:
charts, 132–135
fundamental analysis, 136–137
fundamental indicators, 152–154
generic indicators, 137–141
technical analysis, 135–136
technical indicators, 141–152
Stock exchange, 10
Stock market, generally:
crashes, 8, 147, 166, 169, 187
market corrections, 14
volatility, impact on, 7–8
Stock quotes, components of, 185
Stocks, defined, 6
Stocks and Commodities, 120
Stop limit orders, 188
Stop orders, 187–188
Stop price, 188
Streaming data, investment software, 119–121
Support, 138–139
Support trendline, 138, 158
SureTrade.com, 182
Symbols, 113–114, 120

Taiwan:
country brief, 65–66
index funds, 66–67
Taiwan Fund, Inc., The (TWN), 66–67
Taxation issues, 166
Technical analysis:
characteristics of, 135–136
indicators, *see* Technical indicators
investment software, 124–125
Technical analysts, role of, 135
Technical indicators:
beta, 151–152
Commodity Channel Index, 145–148
function of, generally, 141–142

Technical indicators (*Continued*)
MACD (moving average convergence divergence), 148–150
money flow index, 150–151
moving average, 141–144
oscillators, 141
price oscillator, 144–145
trend, 141
Technology stocks, 168
Templeton China World Fund, Inc. (TCH), 36, 116–117
Templeton funds:
Templeton China World Fund, Inc. (TCH), 36, 116–117
Templeton Russia Fund, Inc. (TRF), 106
Templeton Vietnam and SE Asia Fund (TVF), 75
Templeton Russia Fund, Inc. (TRF), 106
Templeton Vietnam and SE Asia Fund (TVF), 75
Thai Capital Fund, Inc., The (TC), 70
Thai Fund, Inc., The (TTF), 71
Thailand:
country brief, 68–70
index funds, 70–71
Time strategies, basic:
day trading, 162–164
long-term investing, 166–171
medium-term investing, 166
short-term trading/investing, 165–166
Trading, online brokers, 185–186
TradingDirect.com, 183
Trend(s), defined, 87, 141
Turkey:
country brief, 110–111
fundamentals of, 24
index fund, 112
Turkish Investment Fund, Inc., The (TKF), 112, 163–164

U.S. dollar, 136
U.S. Fed, 14

Variation margin call, 170
Vietnam:
country brief, 72–74
index fund, 75
Volatility, 7–8
Volume, stock analysis software:
chart of, 123, 133–134
defined, 115–116, 120

Wall Street Journal, 124
War, impact of, 170
Washington Post, 10, 136
Waterhouse.com, 183
WEBS Index Fund, Inc., 16, 18, 29, 35, 47, 55, 64, 91, 108
WEBS Index Series:
Australia (EWA), 29
Hong Kong (EWH), 35
Japan (EWJ), 47
Malaysia (EWM), 54–55
Mexico (EWW), 91
Singapore (EWS), 63–64
Spain (EWP), 108
WebStreet.com, 183
Weighted moving average, 144
Window on Wall Street, 115, 141, 159, 185
Window on Wall Street Internet Trader Pro 7.0:
chart expert, 125
functions of, generally, 115, 120
Nasdaq Level 2 window, 127–128
Profit "Tester," 125
Time and Sales Window, 127
www.Washingtonpost.com, 126, 158

Yahoo!, 115, 124, 185
Yen, 136